Rick Astle

What
Motivates
God?

Other Books by Rick Astle

The Priority of Kingdom-focused Prayer

The Believer's Guide to Overcoming Temptation

For information on how to order additional copies of Rick Astle's books, or to learn how you can contact him to lead a Prayer or Spiritual Awakening Conference, visit the website of Rick Astle Ministries:

www.RickAstle.com

Rick Astle

What Motivates God?

What Motivates God?
ISBN 978-1-930285-88-0

First Printing

Copyright © 2012 by Rick Astle
Published by The Master Design
     789 State Route 94 E
     Fulton, KY 42041
     bookinfo@masterdesign.org
     www.MasterDesign.org

All Scripture taken from the New King James Version. Copyright © 1982 by Thomas Nelson, Inc. Used by permission. All rights reserved.

Printed by Bethany Press International in the USA.

~ To Donna and John ~

How To Use This Book

 Next to the **Prayer logo** at the close of each chapter is a prayer prompt that can be used by individuals, classes, families and groups during or after the study of that chapter. Intentional, specific prayer should be made using these prompts.

 Next to the **Opened Gift logo** is a description of one of the Gifts of the Holy Spirit that relates well to the particular role of the Father that has been discussed in that chapter. Persons having that Gift will see clear applications to the content of the chapter.

The **Report Card** gives the reader the opportunity to reflect and evaluate, after consideration of the material presented in that chapter. Areas where improvement is needed can be identified, and a corresponding action plan can be created. Small groups will find the report cards useful for discussion of each chapter.

The **Journal of Turning Points** at the end of each chapter is a place for the reader to record dates when personal commitments are made – by either the reader, his family or his church – with dedication to manifest the Father's heart in some manner as prompted by the Holy Spirit from reading the chapter.

PREFACE

To churches already in existence, churches currently being planted, and churches yet to be – these thoughts:

Jesus did not provide a detailed organizational chart for the New Testament Church, although He did lay its foundation by:

- Entrusting the Gospel to it
- Charging that His Gospel be preached to all men
- Providing the twelve apostles for service and teaching
- Empowering its officers for the inclusion and exclusion of fellowship
- Instituting the sacraments of baptism and the Lord's Supper
- Promising to be with it always, even to the end of the world

The foundation-laying work of Jesus Christ for the Church was done once and for all. The building-up of the Church upon that foundation is our responsibility. Our part should be done in the same spirit as His, because it is part of the same work with the foundation-laying.

Jesus said, *"The Son can do nothing of Himself, but what He sees the Father do; for whatever He does, the Son also does in like manner"* (John 5:19). Based on the truth of that statement by our Lord, I have reached the conclusion that the purest way to build *His* Church on *His* foundation, is to represent and express to the world the *heart* — of His, and our, Father.

Myrtle Beach, South Carolina

December, 2011

Table of Contents

INTRODUCTION

The Father's Heart

God wants us to understand Him and to know His heart. Jeremiah 9:24 says, *"But let him who glories glory in this, that he understands and knows Me, that I am the Lord, exercising lovingkindness, judgment, and righteousness in the earth."*

In this introduction you will learn several ways in which God reveals His heart. Of course, even if you master *this* material, you will still have a finite picture of an infinite God. Yet the better we understand His heart, the better we understand what His desires are for His children and for the Church.

God reveals His heart to us in a variety of ways: through His names, through specific references in His Word, through His attributes, through His Son Jesus, and through descriptions from Scripture of what He desires and loves.

God's Names and His Heart

The Hebrew people saw a person's name as descriptive of that person's character or nature. One of the ways we can see and understand God's heart today, is to learn the meaning of His various names that are provided in Scripture.

Listings you may find of the names of God vary, but here are a few of the names He has chosen for Himself and their meaning:

- **"Elohim"** (Mighty one, powerful, Creator God) – Genesis 1:1; Matthew 19:26. Elohim's power has no limit and He will always keep His promises.

- **"El-Roi"** (the God who sees) – Genesis 16:13-14; Hebrews 4:13. El-Roi knows and is alert to our condition, our needs and our circumstances.

- **"Jehovah-Jireh"** (God will provide) – Genesis 22:8; Philippians 4:19. Jehovah-Jireh knows what we need, when we need it, and how to bring it.

- **"Shaddai"** *and* **"El Shaddai"** (power to bless, comfort and make fruitful) – Genesis 28:3. El Shaddai cares for the fatherless and homeless.

- **"Jehovah-Shalom"** (the God of peace) – Judges 6:23-24; Ephesians 2:14-17. Jehovah-Shalom provides peace and harmony in the midst of our circumstances.

- **"Jehovah-Sabbaoth"** (the All-Sovereign One) – 1 Samuel 1:3; Zechariah 4:6-10. With Jehovah-Sabbaoth leading the way and in control, the struggle will not be lost.

- **"Jehovah-Raah"** or **"Jehovah Rohi"** (the Lord is my shepherd) – Psalm 23. Jehovah-Raah provides direction and protection.

- **"Jehovah-Rapha"** (the Lord that heals) – Exodus 15:26. It only takes one touch from Jehovah-Rapha for various types of healing to come.

- **"Jehovah"** (unchanging, keeping His covenant) – Isaiah 42:8; Jeremiah 31:3. Holy Jehovah loves and saves sinners.

- **"Jehovah-Shammah"** (the Lord is there) – Ezekiel 48:35. Jehovah-Shammah is never absent from you, and is Himself all you need.

Specific Scripture References to God's Heart

The Bible names three things that describe the "nature" of God: (a) God is "spirit" (John 4:24), (b) God is "light" (1 John 1:5), and (c) God is "love" (1 John 4:8). But the following verses are examples of places in the Bible where God specifically mentions and explains His "heart":

- **Genesis 8:21** *"Then the Lord said in His heart, 'I will never again curse the ground for man's sake ... nor will I again destroy every living thing as I have done.'"* In God's heart are mercy, grace and patience.

- **1 Samuel 13:14** *"The Lord has sought for Himself a man after His own heart."* Acts 13:22 *"'I have found David the son of Jesse, a man after My own heart, who will do all My will.'"* In God's heart is the search for obedient leaders of great faith – leaders with hearts of integrity, maturity and fidelity.

- **Psalm 33:11** *"The counsel of the Lord stands forever, the plans of His heart to all generations."* In God's heart are Divine counsels that abide and remain firm forever.

- **Jeremiah 3:15** *"'And I will give you shepherds according to My heart, who will feed you with knowledge and understanding.'"* In God's heart is the search for pastors (and civil authorities) who (a) rule and communicate for and like Him in a wise and understanding manner, who (b) understand the nature of the person(s) being looked after, and who (c) recognize the needs, difficulties and best means to satisfy the needs.

- **Jeremiah 48:36** *"'Therefore My heart shall wail like flutes for Moab, and like flutes My heart shall wail for the men of Kir Heres.'"* In God's heart is sympathetic sorrow, here musical in its groans and sighs, for a city and people that had no use for Him and wanted only to shape its own life.

God's Attributes and His Heart

An "attribute" of God is simply anything that is true about Him. Numerous attributes of God are described throughout the Bible, that we might know Him intimately by seeing His heart.

Let's consider the connection between a few of His attributes and His role as Father. God has an infinite number of attributes, so we are limiting our consideration to a dozen.

- **His Glory (He is unlike anything we know.)**
  The glory of God is the sum of all His attributes. He wants His children to know that when they have nothing left but Him, He is enough. Our Heavenly Father wants His children to understand and know Him (Jeremiah 9:24).

- **His Immutability (He is always the same.)**
  Children who were raised in a home with an alcoholic parent know what it is like to live in an unpredictable, unsettled atmosphere. Malachi 3:6 says, *"For I am the Lord, I do not change."* The fact that our Heavenly Father cannot change provides great comfort and stability for His children.

- **His Mercy (He relieves various types of misery.)**
  God's spiritual mercies toward His children manifested when they were dead in sin (Ephesians 2:4-5) and it is His mercy that saves them (Titus 3:5). His sustaining mercies are new every day, sometimes known to His children, sometimes unknown. The Bible says that God is, *"the Father of mercies and God of all comfort"* (2 Corinthians 1:3).

- **His Power (He has the ability to make anything happen.)**
  Jeremiah 32:27 says, *"Behold, I am the Lord, the God of all flesh. Is there anything too hard for me?"* The Bible says a dead man had been in a grave four days when God's Son cried, "Lazarus, come forth," and the dead man emerged. The fact that there is a

limit to the ability of God's children but not to their Father's ability, is a great comfort.

- **His Goodness (He is perfect in His nature.)**
  As Father, God's goodness is demonstrated to His children by the various ways He provides for, gratifies and pleases them. Psalm 145:9 says, *"The Lord is good to all, and His tender mercies are over all His works."* God hears our prayers because He is good.

- **His Wisdom (He has infinite understanding.)**
  The Father's children acquire wisdom through the experiences of life, but God has wisdom by essence. His children are wise in various things, but He is wise in all things. Knowing our lack, He tells His children in James 1:5, *"If any of you lacks wisdom, let him ask of God…and it will be given to him."*

- **His Omniscience (He knows and sees everything.)**
  What a blessing and benefit to the children of God to have a Father who knows all there is to know! As children we experience times of doubt, times of hardship, times of failure and times of weakness. In all circumstances we can turn with confidence to our Heavenly Father because, *"All things are naked and open to the eyes of Him to whom we must give account"* (Hebrews 4:13).

- **His Holiness (He is absolute purity.)**
  In Revelation 15:4 we find these words, *"Who shall not fear You, O Lord, and glorify Your name? For You alone are holy."* Because the Father is holy, all His attributes are holy. Having a Father who is holy, indeed having *anything* that is holy, is something unimaginable to the children of God. We know of nothing to which we can compare holiness. Therefore we must simply rest in the fact that in our

Heavenly Father there is nothing higher or greater or more perfect.

- **His Faithfulness (He cannot deny Himself.)**
Oh, what a blessing it is to God's children that their Father in heaven is faithful to His promises! 2 Timothy 2:13 says, *"If we are faithless, He remains faithful; He cannot deny Himself."* The Father's compassions never fail and are new every morning because of His great faithfulness (Lamentations 3:22-23).

- **His Love (He *is* love.)**
The Father not only "loves," but He is love itself! His love for His children is consistent and does not fluctuate in reaction to their behavior. It is both unmerited and reliable. This is an "alert" love, given while the Father is constantly watching over His children, making corrections when necessary (Proverbs 3:12).

- **His Omnipresence (He is everywhere at once.)**
A child of God cannot do anything or go anywhere without the Father being there. *"'Can anyone hide himself in secret places, so I shall not see him?' says the Lord; 'Do I not fill heaven and earth?' says the Lord"* (Jeremiah 23:24). The Father is nearer to us than our own thoughts!

- **His Patience (He is slow to anger.)**
Earthly fathers are sometimes quick to react angrily, but our Heavenly Father manifests remarkable patience bearing with His children. *"The Lord is gracious and full of compassion, slow to anger and great in mercy,"* says Psalm 145:8. How patiently God handles the sight of wickedness in His children!

What Motivates God?

> ## What Is Clear?
>
> When explaining His *heart* to me, the Father is selecting carefully chosen *truths about Himself* that reveal and explain *specific desires* He has for me and for all men!

Jesus and God's Heart

Only the Son reveals the Father (Matthew 11:27). Jesus spoke out of a unique and intimate relationship with His Father (John 10:30) and manifested and declared the Father to others (John 14:6-11). One of the reasons Jesus came to earth from heaven was to teach us how the Father can be known and trusted. Jesus Christ revealed truth and love to mankind.

In his classic work, *The Training of the Twelve,* A.B. Bruce writes of Jesus, "He spake evermore, in sermon, parable, model prayer, and private conversation, of a Father. Such expressions as "the Father," "my Father," "your Father," were constantly on His tongue; and all He taught concerning God harmonized perfectly with the feelings these expressions were fitted to call forth."

The Father's compassion was revealed in how Jesus responded to the brokenhearted, to sinners, to the religious and to the sick. The Father's forgiving heart and sacrificial love was revealed in looking at Jesus' death on the cross (Luke 23:34).

Here are examples from each of the Gospels that strike me as notable when we seek to see God's heart through His Son:

Matthew 9:36 *"But when He saw the multitudes, He was moved with compassion for them, because they were weary and scattered, like sheep having no shepherd."*

- When Jesus "saw" the multitudes, He saw souls rather than scenery.

- Jesus was "moved" by what He saw. It was more than "feeling sorry for" the people; it was a strong desire to *remove* their suffering.

- All ministry activity should be done with genuine "compassion." We are unlikely to even notice spiritual distress until we have a heart like Jesus.

Matthew 11:29 *"Learn from Me, for I am gentle and lowly in heart."*

- The aorist tense means, "learn once for all." A true disciple is one who has learned due to "contact with Jesus." The heart of Christ is neither overbearing nor haughty nor ambitious – rather it humbly stoops down to us, offering rest and relief. This is the heart, too, of the Father.

- Some teachers can appear outwardly meek and humble without being so in heart. But being "gentle and lowly in heart" is one of the "I AM's" of Jesus.

- It is not any particular "burden" that weighs us down at this moment, but our proud, self-pleasing, rebellious heart. When we get a new, humble, meek heart from Him, our yoke will be easy and our burden light.

- Our Father delights in mercy. The Son still remembers all of the experiences He had on earth, and He welcomes us when we bring our yoke to Him.

- Lowliness is the actual spiritual character of Jesus' person and a huge part of His heart. He left the loftiest state of honor and holiness to come into this world and befriend sinners like you and me.

What Motivates God?

Mark 5:21-43 The Miracle of Raising the Daughter of Jairus from the Dead

The Son's heart is illustrated in this incident by His compassion, His sensitiveness, His indignation, His delicacy and His modesty.

- His Compassion (verse 23)
  "My little daughter." It was a *child* who was ill. Jesus understood what was in the heart of a parent. His was not the heart of the physician or clergyman or church member who merely calls at the house of sorrow as a matter of duty, to be able to say that he has been there.

- His Sensitiveness (verse 23)
  "Come and lay Your hands on her, that she may be healed, and she will live." Jesus was gratified by the faith that Jairus showed. The heart of the Father and of the Son is touched whenever They are regarded with trust or distrust.

- His Indignation (verses 38-40)
  "He... saw a tumult and those who wept and wailed loudly... He said to them, 'Why make this commotion and weep?' ... But when He had put them all outside..." The mourning taking place here was "professional" and insincere, and therefore, unacceptable to the heart of Jesus.

- His Delicacy (verses 40-43)
  "He took the father and mother of the child... and entered where the child was lying... He took the child by the hand... and said that something should be given her to eat." All of this Jesus did with perfect tact, recognizing in His heart that the situation was delicate and full of emotion.

- His Modesty (verse 43)
  "He commanded them strictly that no one should

know it." All kinds of scholarly explanations have been offered through the years as to why Jesus spoke words like this on various occasions, but the best I have seen (when the Word does not provide explanation) is that there were times when Jesus simply disliked having His good deeds made known. Hypocrites have always made a "sensation" of their good works, but that is an attitude far from the heart of God.

Luke 22:15 *"With fervent desire I have desired to eat this Passover with you before I suffer."*

- Known as a "Hebraism" (although here in Greek), the verb used means, "With *great* desire." This desire was due to His deep love for His own.

- The Passover was always meant to remind God's people of the close relationship between God and Israel, going all the way back to the Exodus from Egypt. Now this Passover has to do with the real meaning of Jesus' mission.

- Notice the heart of Jesus here, treasuring these special moments with His brothers and partners. God's heart is for us to work and relate together as a united team (John 17:21) – a team that understands what *He* is doing!

John 17:24 *"Father, I desire that they also whom You gave Me may be with Me..."*

- The verb in the perfect tense refers to a past act with a continuous present effect. Therefore, the reference is to all believers in all ages given to Jesus by God. Those believers yet unborn belong to Jesus, too.

- Jesus and the Father are in perfect accord here, and Their will is expressed for our benefit. Their will is for the whole church to be lifted from earth to heaven. When a world of lost sinners sees unity among believers, it will recognize the divine mission of Jesus. But this unity will only be achieved as believers stay intimate with their exalted Lord and consider His glory.

- God's desire is for all believers to see the wonders of the glory of His Son, and the present tense of the verb indicates a continuous beholding.

- Jesus, for the first time in this prayer, says that He desires or "wills" something. His heart is that He will not be satisfied until all of His blood-bought ones are in His presence. What comfort this is to us! "With me" is the language of love. Jesus is looking forward with anticipation to the embrace of His beloved Bride in the glory that is to be.

Jesus provided numerous revelations of God's heart, saying that God is loving (John 16:27), forgiving (Matthew 6:14), merciful (Luke 6:36), perfect (Matthew 5:48) and generous (Luke 11:13). While praying, Jesus revealed the heart of God by addressing Him as holy (John 17:11) and righteous (John 17:25).

If God seems like a stranger to you, examine the behavior and words of Jesus for a true understanding and concept of your Heavenly Father.

The Loves and Desires of God's Heart

The Bible says God loves *"the stranger, giving him food and clothing"* (Deuteronomy 10:18), *"the righteous"* (Psalm 146:8), *"the world"* (John 3:16), he who loves Jesus (John 14:21,23; 16:27), *"sinners"* (Romans 5:8) and *"a cheerful giver"* (2 Corinthians 9:7).

Anything that God *desires* is clearly a revelation of His heart. The following Scriptures tell us something of what He longs for.

- *"Truth in the inward parts"* (Psalm 51:6). In the most secret moments of thought and behavior (*"For as he thinks in his heart, so is he"* – Proverbs 23:7), God desires perfect sincerity and whole-hearted devotion.

- *"A broken spirit, a broken and a contrite heart"* (Psalm 51:16-17). God desires a heart where pride has been replaced by humility, sorrow and repentance.

- Man (Song of Solomon 7:10). To live so as to be desirable to the Lord is the highest purpose of a believer's life. To be able to say, *"His desire is toward me,"* brings ultimate satisfaction.

- *"Mercy"* (Hosea 6:6). Referenced twice by Jesus speaking to the Pharisees (Matthew 9:13; 12:7), making the point that ritual is of no value apart from steadfast love and true devotion leading to maturity.

- For *"all men to be saved"* (1 Timothy 2:4). This is the *reason* why believers should pray fervently for those who are lost. In doing so, we are praying according to His will and to the desire of His heart.

The Father's Daily Agenda

In eastern thought, the father was motivated by (and assumed all responsibility for) providing his children with the most important needs of life. Similarly, our Heavenly Father performs the following eight roles each and every day. His desire to perform these roles *perfectly* in the life of His children is what "motivates" Him.

1. To **care (Psalm 68:5)**
   "A father of the fatherless, a defender of widows."
2. To **correct (Proverbs 3:12)**

"For whom the Lord loves He corrects, just as a father the son in whom he delights."

3. To **teach** (Job 36:22)
   "Behold, God is exalted by His power; Who teaches like Him?"

4. To **listen** (Psalm 94:9)
   "He who planted the ear, shall He not hear?"

5. To **protect** (John 10:29)
   "My Father, who has given them to Me, is greater than all; and no one is able to snatch them out of My Father's hand."

6. To **lead** (Jeremiah 31:9)
   "They shall come with weeping, and with supplications I will lead them... for I am a Father to Israel."

7. To **forgive** (Ephesians 4:32)
   "Forgiving one another, even as God in Christ forgave you."

8. To **love** (John 3:16)
   "For God so loved the world that He gave His only begotten Son..."

Why would God reveal His heart? So that *our* hearts can be in tune with *His.* So that we can place *our* priorities as a family and as the Church where *He* is focused. So that *we* can be working where *He* is working. So that *our* will can become the same as *His* will.

If God's primary role is to be a perfect Father, then our primary function should be to join Him as He performs that role. If the Church views God as a Father, it should base its ministries around God's heart and around what God is doing.

In the chapters that follow, you will learn how the believer, the family and the church can have the same daily agenda as the Father.

What Should I Do Before I Read The Rest Of This Book?

Slowly review and meditate over the material in this introdution. Be willing to let the Father change your heart to be more like His. Note the specific areas where your heart is *unlike* God's, and invite the Holy Spirit to go to work!

What Motivates God?

Notes On "The Father's Heart"

_____

_____

_____

_____

_____

_____

_____

_____

_____

_____

_____

_____

_____

_____

_____

_____

_____

_____

Journal Of Turning Points

*"To him who knows to do good and does not do it,
to him it is sin." (James 4:17)*

DATE | COMMITMENT

_____

_____

_____

_____

_____

"*People want to know how much you care before they care how much you know.*"

- James F. Hind

Chapter One

Caring from The Father's Heart

The Anatomy of Caring

A minister friend of mine often challenges believers by asking them whether they view people as scenery, machinery or souls. In other words, when we see people, do they blend in with the trees, traffic or concrete? Are people simply "items" that are in place to benefit us personally in some way? Or do we look at those around us with awareness that they are each precious souls for whom Jesus died? Caring is the opposite of seeing people as "machinery" that we can use for the purpose of satisfying our own selfish desires.

The late South African freelance photographer, Kevin Carter, won the Pulitzer Prize for a disturbing photo he took in 1993 during the famine in Sudan. He described how he discovered a starving little girl alone out in the bush, who was literally crawling towards a United Nations food camp located about a kilometer away. As Carter crouched to photograph the child, a vulture landed in view and remained nearby for about twenty minutes waiting for the girl to die.

After taking his pictures of the child and the bird, to his credit, Kevin Carter chased the vulture away. But the little girl resumed her struggle without receiving any help from the satisfied photographer. His work completed, Carter walked away. The fate of the child is unknown.

Caring involves responsibility.

Furthermore, once we are in the act of caring for someone, there are a number of things we need to consider, such as:

Being *knowledgeable* of the other's needs
Being *patient* with the other's confusion or with slow

1

progress (theirs or ours)
Being *honest* about the other's circumstances
Being *humble* about the need to learn while caring for the other
Being *aware* that caring may or may not be reciprocated
Being *willing* to empathize with the other
Being *capable* of helping the other

The person for whom we are caring, then, becomes an extension of ourselves - a process perfectly modeled through the manner in which God our Father cares for us.

The Father's Agenda

"A father of the fatherless, a defender of widows, is God in His holy habitation."

– Psalm 68:5

It is a comfort to know that God watches over us from His seat in the highest heaven. But our Heavenly Father further blesses us in that His heart for us is to not only "observe," but to *care enough to act* on His observation of our need. Psalm 146:9 says He "*relieves*" the fatherless and widow. Concerning the fatherless, Psalm 10:14 says God is their "*helper.*"

If we are not careful, Christians can react to the sight of spiritual suffering in the same manner that photographer Kevin Carter reacted to seeing a starving child. Carter was so occupied with the mechanics of being a good photographer that he missed the more important opportunity – as do we, when we are so busy with the mechanics of being a good Christian that we fail to give lost people the bread of life.

Scripture mentions orphans and widows when describing not only the recipients of the Father's attention and care, but also when describing "*pure and undefiled religion before God and the Father*" (James 1:27). (To clarify, "*reli-*

2

gion" in this verse, refers to religious *"service"* and *"God and the Father"* to our God and Father.)

Our purpose is not to search a concordance for all references to the "fatherless" and to "widows." The fatherless and widows are among the brokenhearted, the sorrowful and those whose homes and emotions have been shattered. We must also minister to the homeless, single parents, the poor, the stranger and others who are among *"the least of these"* referred to by our Lord Jesus in Matthew 25:40.

When it comes to caring, then, what does the Bible say is on the Father's agenda?

Providing for those who have no source of help or comfort, emotionally or physically has always been on the Father's agenda. That is why the Jewish society emphasized a moral responsibility to care for them (Exodus 22:22; Deuteronomy Chapters 10, 14, 16, 24, 26, 27). The Father's Agenda is to relieve people who, regardless of their circumstances, need special care through a display of Christian love.

Caring about the souls of all men is always on God's agenda. Paul modeled how to care for others when we share the gospel (1 Corinthians 9:19-23). We are saved by His *"grace"* (Ephesians 2:8; Titus 2:11) - a word in Greek that conveys the idea of *benevolence.*

On the Father's agenda is **shepherding *"for His name's sake"*** (Psalm 23:3). It is His *nature* to perfectly care for and comfort His sheep. Jesus emphasized His Father's commitment to caring and providing, and urged us not to be anxious about earthly needs (Matthew 6:8, 26, 30, 32; Luke 12:30).

While being a true disciple of Jesus Christ means much more than merely performing works of charity, it is clear that the Church must neither overlook nor neglect to help those who are *"weary and scattered, like sheep having no shepherd*" (Matthew 9:36). The Church, like Jesus, should be "*moved with* **compassion**" when observing and ministering to people in need.

The word "compassion" is derived from the Latin words *com* (with, together) and *pati* (to suffer, to hurt). When you have compassion for someone, you "suffer with" a person in need or "hurt together" with a person in pain. "Church Prayer Meeting" should include compassionate intercessory prayer for needy ones who are on the Father's heart. Jeremiah 3:15 speaks of "*shepherds according to My heart*" who care enough for the sheep to feed them "*with knowledge and understanding.*"

According to James 1:27, we minister best to the afflicted as the result of an actual "***visit***" where "*their affliction*" can be physically observed and comfort can be personally provided. "Church Visitation" should include intentional visits to "the least of these" and to the lost, rather than merely to "prospects" for church membership. When we visit the sick and those in prison, we meet Jesus there (Matthew 25:36). This type of visit is actually an act of *worship* that shows respect for and is seen by "*God and the Father.*" Caring from the Father's heart is much more for God's eyes than man's eyes.

A "caring church member" is not necessarily saved! Use discretion regarding the church member who is constantly drawing attention to his own charitable visits and deeds. There are people (whether involved or uninvolved in church life) who focus on their "external" world as a substitute for dealing with their "internal" world. The purity of our "*religion*" depends upon the *motivation* of our good works, and must be undefiled by self-promotion, hypocrisy or inconsistency.

Caring from the Father's heart includes making every effort to preserve **unity** in the church. Acts 6:1 describes not only a situation where "*widows were neglected,*" but also a situation where a *"complaint"* threatened to bring division and discord within the fellowship. Continuous prayer should be offered for and careful attention given to preserve something as precious as unity in the church. 1 Corinthians 12:25 declares that members in the body *"should have the same care for one another"* and that there should be no *"schism."*

Make certain that your church is caring from the Father's heart as it ministers to the special needs of your church family, and of families in the community. Well-equipped and staffed nurseries and children's programs, child care, day care, church media resources, mother's day out, fellowship opportunities, recreational activities, and divorced and single parent ministries are only a few examples of how your church can care from the Father's heart.

What Do You See?

I have met folks who say that they enjoy "people watching" at the shopping malls. We know that appearances can be deceiving. But as you observe people in various contexts, as you look randomly at their countenance and their behavior, how would you describe them?

Reentering the United States after spending some time abroad, the American traveler notices things that previously have not captured his attention. The caring and observant person who refuses to see people merely as "scenery," notices the grim monotony and telling story of American facial expressions that reveal such prevailing feelings as confusion, sadness, aloofness, anger, frustration, indifference and perhaps the most common – loneliness and withdrawal.

"I Can't Get No Satisfaction" is not only a rock song from the 1960's - it is a phrase that I believe still describes how many millions of Americans actually feel. Greedy advertisers capitalize on this discontent, by promoting products (using stereotyped symbols of fun such as running through fields, strolling on beaches, dancing, drinking, singing, and smiling with artificially whitened teeth) that only leave people further disappointed and unsatisfied.

Please understand that when I use the word "loneliness," I am not referring to the occasional and normal desire for "privacy." Rather I am speaking of the longing, even the eagerness to be shut off, left alone and isolated. John Lennon and Paul McCartney observantly asked through a song years ago, "All the lonely people – where do they all come from?" Today, it is as though we are actually in *pursuit* of loneliness!

It is alarming that the pursuit of loneliness has made its way into the Church. When given the opportunity to participate in Christian fellowship *outside one's own church walls*, too many of today's pastors and church members say, "Thanks, but no thanks." Most "pastors' conferences" (meetings that provide the opportunity for fellowship among local ministers) are poorly attended, and a large number of church members have only a few Christian friends that attend church "somewhere else." We view relationships as too time consuming, sticky, unsafe, risky – even bothersome.

Why are so many people pursuing loneliness and isolation? Psychologists tell us that there are "emotional" influences that can create and maintain loneliness. Perhaps when we are strangers to our own selves, we prefer to be strangers to others as well. People who feel out of touch with themselves are not always anxious to touch others.

And then there is the matter of self-esteem. Individuals with a very *low* opinion of themselves, tend to withdraw from others rather than face embarrassment. Individuals with a very *high* opinion of themselves, tend to withdraw from others rather than be annoyed by "all the idiots out there."

In addition, psychologists tell us that there are "social" influences that can increase our loneliness. Technology has produced such things as wide-screen television, video games, DVDs, computers and iPads that can "entertain" us for hours. As helpful as these devices can be, the amount of time spent using them severely limits time for personal relationships. Widespread mobility causes many people to shy away from close friendships in order to avoid painful separations. For a number of years now, millions of Americans have lived without knowing even the first name of their next-door neighbor.

Paul Tournier, the Swiss counselor, wrote down some thoughts about loneliness shortly after World War II. His ideas are surprisingly relevant for today. According to Tournier, we have developed *"parliamentary attitudes* in which we see life as a big tournament with success as the winner's prize and competition as a way of life; *independent attitudes* which cause us to act as if we were each rugged individualists, absolutely autonomous, independent of God and of others; *possessive attitudes* by which we are driven to get what we can for ourselves; and *demanding attitudes* which cause us to fight for our rights and to demand 'fairness.'"

If Tournier is right, it is easy to see how these kinds of attitudes would lead us to use other people mainly as machinery to satisfy our own desires – resulting eventually in our driving people away.

Caring Through Intercession

Turn to Acts Chapter 12 and you will read one of my favorite places in the Bible that illustrates the power of God manifesting as the result of intercessory prayer. What happened when the church prayed strenuously, earnestly, specifically and constantly for Peter while he was in prison, was nothing short of miraculous! Verse 7 says that *"Chains fell off his hands*" (*noiselessly,* according to the most accurate translation!), and verse 10 says that the heavy, iron city gate "*opened to them of its own accord.*"

On the one hand we have a prison, four squads of soldiers, chains, prison guards and a huge iron gate – and on the other hand we have a church *caring* for Peter through intercessory prayer! Notice the contrast! Notice the conflict and the warfare! Notice the outcome!

There are three important aspects of caring through intercessory prayer worthy of consideration. *First*, understand the *truths* about intercessory prayer. Here is what we know:

- Intercession may be either "for" (1 Timothy 2:1, 2) or "against" (Romans 11:2) a thing, person or nation.

- Intercession provides sweet fellowship with the Holy Spirit (Romans 8:26, 27).

- Intercession is strenuous work (Romans 15:30; Colossians 4:12)

- Intercession is serving (Mark 10:44, 45)

- Intercession is warfare (Luke 22:39-44)

- Intercession is weeping (Psalm 126:5, 6)

- Intercession is obedience (1 Samuel 12:23)

Second, understand the *benefits* of intercessory prayer.

(1) **Concerning Missions Education**. For example, consider the value of intercessory prayer to your children and grandchildren as they are led during family devotion times to pray concerning missionaries, conflict, or disasters around the world. History and geography become more interesting to them while they care through intercession for real people in various lo-

cations. Teach them about great intercessors such as Hudson Taylor (China), David Livingstone (Africa), and William Carey (India), who were each students of the map.

Let's get you started! Saut d' Eau (pronounced SO-toe), Haiti, is a small village of about 8,000 people. Located north of Port au Prince, I had never heard of this place until I visited there in 2011. Saut d' Eau is known as "the devil's throne on earth" because of visits there by many thousands of people from all over the world who practice voodoo. *Please pause now and intercede for pastors and missionaries who live and minister in and around Saut d' Eau, Haiti.*

(2) **Concerning Mankind.** Whenever we care enough to pray for the peoples of the world, we realize the importance of knowing something about them. We begin to look upon men as Jesus looks upon them. Souls are souls everywhere, no matter what language is spoken, no matter what color the skin, no matter what religion they embrace. Since people are of great importance to the Father, we should seek to learn as much as we can about all men.

(3) **Concerning the Intercessor.** The prayer that reaches heaven is a work of the Holy Spirit. Whatever gain other people may receive from our intercession, we receive the greater blessing as the Spirit is doing His perfecting work in us. Praying for those who are hard to love (Matthew 5:44; Luke 23:34) is evidence of God at work in us. Caring intercession brings us to know the Father, the Son, the Spirit, the Bible, ourselves, and mankind as we could scarcely know them in any other way.

Third, understand the ***method*** of intercessory prayer. Charles L. Allen, in his book, *All Things Are Possible Through Prayer*, suggests these five steps:

1. Pray *definitely* for that one person or concern. Identify the need as specifically as possible.

2. *Think of God* while you hold that particular person in mind. Think of a particular scene in the life of Christ that corresponds to that need.

3. Think of your prayer as *lifting that person or concern into the presence of the Father.* You are supplying the human cooperation necessary for bringing that person and God together.

4. *Tell God what is on your heart.* Pray positively.

5. *Be faithful and persistent.* Keep praying until God's answer comes.

Caring Through Missions

Missions begins in the home. Family devotion and worship times provide excellent opportunities to pray for people on mission in this country and throughout the world. Discuss family members' answers to this question: "Would a lost person who spent a week living in our home see and hear the Father's heart by watching the way we behave, speak, make decisions and prioritize?"

How can your family express the Father's heart to your neighbors? Children can raise money for family mission projects by setting up a refreshment stand for people walking, jogging or bicycling. Members of your family can take turns walking throughout your area praying for the salvation of and blessing on the occupants of each house. Invite a neighbor to dinner who has recently lost his/her job, or who is a widow or widower.

How about a family piggy bank for missions? Watch with praise and anticipation as the container fills up to capacity and someone on the mission field is about to be blessed.

What about using one week of annual family vacation time for a family mission trip, local or abroad. Let the family pray together about where to visit, and pray for the people in that location long before you leave on the trip. When you go on "normal" family vacations, dedicate one of the days at your location for mission activity (distributing gospel tracts, praying on-site, street evangelism, connecting with a local missions organization, etc.).

The Vinedresser Caring for The Branch

Jesus said that His Father is the Vinedresser or "husband-man" (John 15:1). Whether the branch is a man or woman, the Father is the husband of the branch. He cares for the branch out of His complete understanding of human need.

When we have opportunities to care for others, it is important that we show the patience, compassion and knowledge of the Vinedresser. In her classic book, *Common Human Needs*, Charlotte Towle made this powerful statement that all of us should remember as we observe, and seek to understand, human behavior: "No matter how unusual an individual's behavior may seem to us, it has its rational foundation, its logic. His behavior, like ours, is serving him some useful purpose in the maintenance of a kind of equilibrium, that is, a state of comfort in his life."

Every branch is fighting a battle. The Vinedresser understands, and compassionately addresses that fact.

How can a believer express the Father's heart by caring? Luke 6:36 says that we are to *"be merciful, just as your Father also is merciful."* This merciful behavior is more often "intentional" than spontaneous, and is not intended to permanently fix or repair anyone or anything. Rather it is intended to show the compassion of a caring Father.

Search the newspaper or watch the news to learn of individuals in your area who are suffering, and bring them a basket of homemade bread or cookies with a Scripture verse attached. Take a personal field trip to a nursing home or assisted living facility, and sit down and talk with a lonely person. Bring a meal to an elderly neighbor who lives alone and pray with them before you leave.

Knock on a neighbor's door and ask if there is a concern that you can pray about for them; visit again in a week or so and get an update regarding their concern. Answer the question, "Who are the down-and-out in my community?" and *connect compassionately* with these people under the prompting of the Holy Spirit.

Missions is not *limited* to "trips," but be open to going somewhere outside your comfort zone if the Holy Spirit is prompting. Try not to say or think, "Anywhere but Africa! Anywhere but China! (Hello, Bahamas!)" etc. Particularly if you have health concerns, you may wish to minister alongside family or friends if "trips" are new to you. Your pastor should be able to assist you with connecting to the proper mission groups, agencies or organizations as you pray.

> **What Is Clear?**
>
> I need to see the fields that are already white for harvest, with people who are becoming more and more withdrawn and in need of care from the Father's heart!

 Church unity is something worth praying for. Do not wait until the fighting breaks out to pray for unity! The enemy will be much less apt to carry out a sneak attack if he sees that there are intercessors already posted at the gate.

Think about the people you care for deeply. Pray that you will recognize if you are neglecting any responsibility toward them. Remember that caring with the Father's heart carries with it the responsibility of fervent prayer.

If you have the Spiritual Gift of Mercy (Romans 12:8) your role in the church is to express the compassion of the Father's heart in a variety of ways. You have the ability to feel genuine empathy and compassion for individuals who are suffering physically, emotionally or spiritually. You act with supernatural ability on the opportunity to alleviate suffering.

Believers with the Spiritual Gift of Mercy feel supernaturally motivated to take part in or to establish ministries such as: Benevolence ministry, Food closet, Hospital visitation, Crisis pregnancy ministry, Homeless ministry, Widows/widowers ministry, Single parent ministry, Prison ministry, Senior adult ministry and Roadside prayer ministry.

What Motivates God?

Usually Does
Too Often Does Not

PERSONAL REPORT CARD

____ ____ Sees people as souls and prays for their salvation

____ ____ Provides for those who have no source of help or comfort

____ ____ Intentionally seeks, finds and ministers to the needy

____ ____ Regularly intercedes in prayer for ministers and missionaries

FAMILY REPORT CARD

____ ____ Has family devotion time at home when we pray for and learn about missionary work

____ ____ Gives money to support missions

____ ____ Prayerfully considers taking part in local and distant mission projects

____ ____ Demonstrates the Father's heart by how we treat one another at our house

CHURCH REPORT CARD

____ ____ Prays for the needy and lost, as much as for the physically sick

____ ____ Intentionally ministers to orphans, widows and the needy

____ ____ Pastor and leaders work hard to keep the church members unified, cared for and comforted

____ ____ Financially and physically supports mission work generously, both locally and abroad

Notes On "Caring from The Father's Heart"

_____

_____

_____

_____

_____

_____

_____

_____

_____

_____

_____

_____

_____

_____

_____

_____

_____

_____

Journal Of Turning Points

*"To him who knows to do good and does not do it,
to him it is sin."* *(James 4:17)*

DATE | COMMITMENT

_____

_____

_____

_____

_____

"Most people when they come to you for advice, come to have their own opinions strengthened, not corrected."

- Josh Billings

Chapter Two

Correcting from The Father's Heart

Discipline and Correction

Well this is going to be a fun chapter to read, right? Actually, it may be more rewarding than you think – for there is much for the growing Christian to learn on this subject, even though from childhood we have attached a negative meaning to these words. So, be receptive! Here we go.

The Bible describes disciplinary actions and corrective measures that are made in the lives of men (and nations) by God the Father. In the Old Testament, emphasis is placed on the process of not only reproof but also of education in the family. For example, fathers had the responsibility to educate their sons in the traditions of the chosen people and in the commandments of the law. In the New Testament, the challenges and difficulties that come to God's people are seen more often as indications of God's fatherly training. Yet we still see the picture of the earthly father relating to his children in the home (Ephesians 6:4).

Sometimes earthly parents use threats like, "If you do that one more time..." or "Just wait until your dad gets home..." or "I'm going to count to three..." - and then they don't follow through. This often results in the child not listening.

We should not misinterpret the fact that God's preference is to redeem rather than to punish. But our Heavenly Father doesn't make "empty threats;" He follows through with what He says He will do! Because He is a loving Father, He will bring the discipline and correction. And when He does, we should accept it as a sign of His love. Even so, *and praise His name, "He has not dealt with us according to our sins, nor punished us according to our iniquities*" (Psalm 103:10).

A type of correction is "restoration," described in Galatians 6:1 by Paul using a hypothetical situation. The person referred to in this verse has not sinned deliberately or habitually, but has rather been "*overtaken,*" or surprised, in trespass (sin). It is like the driver of a vehicle who, due to lack of watchfulness or carelessness, travels too fast around a curve in the road and ends up in a ditch. His brothers and sisters in Christ are to come to the rescue.

"Restore" in this context has the same meaning as to mend a net, or to set a broken bone. Christians, therefore, should remember these seven truths when restoring a brother:

- The right *motive* is that of *helping* this person
- The right *goal* is that of *loving* this person
- The right *tool* to use (with compassion) is the *Bible*
- The right *attitude* is that of *humility and meekness*, realizing that we, too, may fall when tempted
- The right *perspective* is that of *specks and planks* (see Matthew 7:3)
- The right *behavior* is that of *Christian grace*, rather than Christian cannibalism (see Galatians 5:15)
- The right *conclusion* is that of *forgiving* this person

The Father's Heart Regarding Control of The Church

This is a difficult chapter for me to write. I realize that I will need to be very specific, and that in doing so, I will be critical of some things that are dear to my heart. It pains me to have to point out some of these things so bluntly. But it is necessary to do so, because lack of discernment, lack of care, and lack of action concerning these matters is having a negative impact on the Church we all love.

The "Report Cards" found at the close of each chapter in this book are designed to serve as a step toward accountability. From the pulpit to the pew, we have gradually made our way from the point of admitting the *truth* that "nobody's perfect" and "all have sinned," to the point of embracing the *lie* that "nobody's accountable." Surely the Father's heart is grieved over this decline.

Regarding the pulpit, a number of pastors are telling their congregations that the Bible says the pastor is "accountable *only* to God" (chapter and verse, please?) when in reality, some of these pastors (a) feel insecure and can't handle even truthful criticism that is shared lovingly by fellow minister friends or compassionate church members, or (b) want to be the unchallenged church boss with the power, or (c) all of the above.

Unfortunately, the "I answer only to God" declaration is too often just a convenient way for legalistic or insecure pastors to maintain control. Holy Spirit conviction followed by repentance is needed in these circumstances. Pastors are not called to be lords of the sheep. They are humble servants of the King, called to imitate the chief Shepherd.

We should not pose as profound people; God became a Baby! The greatest frauds, the shallowest individuals we have ever known – are we. We do well to remember Paul's words recorded in Romans 12:3: "*For I say, through the grace given to me, to everyone who is among you, not to think of himself more highly than he ought to think, but to think soberly.*"

Just as prevalent as the dictatorial pastor, and just as harmful, is the flock-pleasing pastor whose focus is on keeping the flock satisfied and happy. Peace at any price translates into job security for these leaders. I conversed with one such pastor some time ago and listened to him boastfully say of his congregation, "They will do anything I ask of them." I remember thinking to myself, "But I wonder if they will do anything *Jesus* asks of them."

Regarding behavior in the pew, my observation is that local church members are often more desirous to win an argument or a church vote than they are to win (*"gain"*) a brother (Matthew 18:15). A church operating with the Father's heart is a church "winning" the lost (1 Corinthians 9:19-22), as well as "winning" fellow brothers and sisters.

As with some occupants of the pulpit, some occupants of the pew have controlling spirits. I know quite a number of churches that are clearly "family owned and operated." As soon as the pastor rubs a member of the controlling family the wrong way, his remaining days in the pulpit are numbered. *Also guilty are the spiritually weak church members who passively allow unjustified forced terminations to happen!*

Relationships

The whole allegory of the Vineyard in John Chapter 15 is about relationships. When there is a breakdown in the relationship between the branch and the Vine, the result will be a breakdown in the relationship of one branch to another. The Father "rents" His vineyard to tenants, and demands an accounting from them (Mark 12:1-12; Matthew 20:1-16; 21:33-43). Therefore it is appropriate as we consider the church, to examine two vitally important areas where the body of Christ can demonstrate weakness concerning how we treat one another.

Space does not permit me to provide a long discourse on the well-known passage regarding church discipline given by our Lord and recorded in Matthew 18:15-35. The commentaries devote thousands of pages to it. But I do want to comment at this time on a lesser-known verse, found in 1 Timothy 3:15: "*I write so that you may know how you ought to conduct yourself in the house of God, which is the church of the living God, the pillar and ground of the truth."*

What does it mean, that the church is *"the pillar and ground of the truth?"* We know that the purpose of a pillar is to "support" something. This short statement makes the powerful declaration that *actual truth leans upon the Church for support!* The church of Jesus Christ is supposed to consist of people who are truthful and honest, thus providing the support for what is truth.

Let this powerful declaration from God's Word "sink in." Not the universities, not the governments, not the social movements of the world – only the Christian Church has this grave responsibility! Now, here's the concern before us. When church members behave in a worldly manner (which they will), and are not Scripturally disciplined through the church, *"the pillar and ground of the truth"* becomes a lie personified!

And so I have chosen to highlight this verse (rather than the verses in the eighteenth chapter of Matthew), because 1 Timothy 3:15 plainly declares the *reason why* we cannot afford to ignore the responsibility of lovingly administering church discipline when appropriate. There is simply too much at stake – *regardless of how much the offender may contribute to the church financially or through service.*

From the church family we move now to the home, and consider two particular verses.

(1) Ephesians 6:4

Training and admonition *"Of the Lord"* reminds fathers to correct and instruct their children:

- for *Him*, according to *His* will, and in *His* spirit
- that they may know, worship and love *Him*
- that they may be prepared to obey and serve *Him* understanding *His* will for their lives

23

- that they would exhibit *His* order and self-control
- that they would know right from wrong according to *His* Word
- remembering that they are a heritage from *Him* (Psalm 127:3)

Such is the duty of the father toward the child from infancy to maturity. It should be stated that the father will not have a clue as to how to do all of the above unless he is, himself, abiding in the Vine.

(2) Proverbs 22:6

What is the meaning of the phrase, "*the way he should go*"? That "*way*" is found in Jesus Himself, "*the way, the truth, and the life*" (John 14:6). As parents, we are to "*walk in Him*" (Colossians 2:6), setting the example for our children to do the same. The Father's method of correction and training consists of both show *and* tell.

Parents who view the way of the Lord as "a" way instead of "*the*" way, will be among the parents who are puzzled when their children are grown and demonstrate poor behavior. The body of Christ needs more fathers and mothers who love parenting *only* in the spiritual realm. Mix in the ways of the world with your spiritual training, and you lose the promise. Training children from the Father's heart must include such loving expressions as discipline, supervision, counsel, nurture and reproof.

"*The way he should go*" includes not just "reading" the Bible, but also "studying" and "knowing" the Bible at an early age. 2 Timothy 3:15 says, "*And that from childhood you have known the Holy Scriptures, which are able to make you wise for salvation through faith which is in Christ Jesus.*" In the following verse 16, Paul names "*instruction in righteousness*" as one of the four major functions of Holy Scripture. Paul is referring here to how God's Holy Word provides education and discipline that leads to righteous living.

To conclude, the parent must (a) make "*the way he should go*" his one goal in the child's training, and (b) insure that "*the way he should go*" is in complete accordance with God's Word.

Interpreting the Father's Correction

"For whom the Lord loves He corrects, just as a father the son in whom he delights."

– Proverbs 3:12

The mature believer reacts to the Father's correction with a *Scriptural* interpretation and understanding. When you realize that the Vinedresser is at work in your life, there are certain truths from God's Word that you should remember:

- **You need the correction, or He wouldn't be giving it.** Psalm 119:75: "*I know, O Lord, that your judgments are right, and that in faithfulness You have afflicted me.*"

- **He loves you, or He wouldn't be correcting you.** Revelation 3:19: "*As many as I love, I rebuke and chasten. Therefore be zealous and repent.*"

- **There is no reason to become discouraged when He corrects you**. Hebrews 12:5: "*My son, do not despise the chastening of the Lord, nor be discouraged when you are rebuked by Him.*"

- **There is no gain in trying to escape the correction**. Hebrews 12:7: "*If you endure chastening, God deals with you as with sons; for what son is there whom a father does not chasten?*"

- **There is a great reward after correction**. Hebrews 12:10: "*That we may be partakers of His holiness.*"

And what can the child expect from this perfect, loving Father who provides correction? He can expect the Father to know his need, to apply the discipline properly, to know the right timing, to use the appropriate means, to exercise the suitable intensity, and to use the most effective instrument!

We can expect these things from the Father because only excellence can proceed from Him (Psalm 150:2), along with skill and attention to detail. He is merciful over His entire creation (Psalm 145:9). No matter how circumstances may appear, all of the Father's acts are wrought in perfect wisdom. We are like young plants that are easily frustrated and don't like to be disturbed. Our task, therefore, is to rely on the Father's goodness, wisdom and power.

"My Father is the Vinedresser" (John 15:1)

Jesus made it clear that He could do nothing *"of Himself"* (John 5:19). Every day, Jesus depended on the Father for everything – and so it is with the **VINE** being dependent upon the **VINEDRESSER**. Branches (you and I) are to trust the Father for provision and protection in the same way that Jesus trusted Him. Isaiah 27:2 speaks of, *"A vineyard of red wine. I the Lord, keep it, I water it every moment; lest any hurt it, I keep it night and day."*

Without a **BRANCH** (verse 2), a Vine can bear no fruit. The vine is great and strong; the branch is small, weak and in constant need of strength from the vine. Therefore, the challenge to the branch is restful surrender, seeking and knowing nothing but the Vine.

The Vinedresser expects the branch to **BEAR FRUIT** (verse 2) for the growth of His kingdom. All believers, as branches, "bear" the fruit - but we do not *generate* it. We are neither the Vine nor the fruit; we are just the "go-between."

Fruit refers to a variety of *things that glorify the Father*. For example, we glorify God when the *"fruit of the Spirit"* (see Galatians 5:22-23) manifests within us. The Father is also glorified when we *"maintain good works"* (Titus 3:14).

But perhaps the best and most lasting fruit ever produced is the fruit of soul winning (Proverbs 11:30).

Andrew Murray, in his classic work, *The True Vine*, writes, "Christ and the believer, the heavenly Vine and the branch, have equally their place in the world exclusively for one purpose: to carry God's saving love to men. The one object of my being a branch, the one mark of my being a true branch, the one condition of my abiding and growing strong, is that I bear the fruit of the heavenly Vine for dying men to eat and live."

In order to make the branch more fruitful, the Father **PRUNES** (verse 2) the branch. Winemakers will tell you that pruning is the very heart of grape growing and the process on which everything else depends. Getting the best out of a grapevine usually means going against the natural tendencies of the plant. Yet even if the growth of the branch has been abundant, the need *increases* for pruning.

Pruning is often painful and that pain will be felt in an *identifiable place*! If you are under conviction for being a fruitless branch, confess that sin or hindrance so that you can bear fruit for the glory of God. Hindrances to life and growth may include the cares of life, the influence of wealth, or the lusts of the flesh.

The Vinedresser wants you to reach your *greatest potential*, so His knife is necessary for your good and for His glory. Remember: The desire of the Father's heart is to help you choose what is *best* over what is "good." Cutting away those "lesser priorities" makes room for God to receive more glory.

There is enough "self" in even the best of branches to warrant the "**PRUNING-KNIFE**." The Vinedresser's knife performs functions very much like those of the Word of God: *"sharper than any two-edged sword"* (Hebrews 4:12), it is *"profitable for"* both correction and instruction (2 Timothy 3:16).

It is imperative that we understand (and gratefully receive with child-like surrender) pruning from the Vinedresser. No communion is so close, so fruitful – seldom is Jesus more precious to us and His love more sweet – than in the experience of the Father's pruning. At the end of the day, what can it all mean but that *God is motivated by being our perfect Father!*

Pruning is the process through which the Vinedresser cuts things out of our lives, so that we will **BEAR MORE FRUIT** (verse 2), even **MUCH FRUIT** (verse 5). Notice that this challenge is to the branch that is *already bearing fruit!* Clearly the Vinedresser would not have us become content, satisfied or proud with merely "some" fruit.

To be more specific, we see two types of circumstances in which pruning takes place. The first circumstance is when healthy branches that are currently bearing fruit are pruned so that they can produce "more" fruit, or even "much" fruit. The second circumstance is when the Vinedresser **TAKES AWAY** (verse 2) the fruitless branch if necessary, resulting in loss of reward (not loss of salvation, if abiding in the Vine) - because a fruitless branch is, in reality, a shame to the Vinedresser.

Since only the Father *perfectly* sees and *justly* evaluates the hearts and works of men, we do better leaving this matter to Him, while making sure that we are abiding in the Vine. Said Corrie Ten Boom commenting on this very passage: "Like some railway tickets in America, I am 'Not good if detached.'"

The Vinedresser is the one who owns or keeps the vineyard. He sows, cultivates, prunes and longs for abundant fruit. One of His specific jobs is to make sure that His branches don't get covered in dirt (sin). Depending on how the branch responds to early correction attempts (some branches respond differently than others), the Father may proceed to demonstrate His care through **CHASTENING** or spiritual discipline.

Chastening is a *love* word; all suffering is not chastening. The very same reprimand may fall on two individuals, and be in the one case "judgment" while in the other case "love." Jeremiah 2:30 describes the child who does not receive correction as he should: "*In vain I have chastened your children; they received no correction.*" Chastening is the father correcting his child for the purpose of education, with the hope that it will be *received* as such.

Yes, it may be painful! Hebrews 12:11 says, "*Now no chastening seems to be joyful for the present, but painful; nevertheless, afterward it yields the peaceable fruit of righteousness to those who have been trained by it.*" This cleansing encourages repentance. Remember, the discipline ceases when specific sin is abandoned.

So let us do well in receiving both the Father's pruning and chastening! Here is how Paul put it all in perspective: "*But what things were gain to me, these I have counted loss for Christ. Yet indeed I also count all things loss for the excellence of the knowledge of Christ Jesus my Lord, for whom I have suffered the loss of all things, and count them as rubbish, that I may gain Christ*" (Philippians 3:7-8).

Jesus made it clear to His disciples that He expects both a high *quantity* and a high *quality* fruit that will ensure the preservation of the Church until the end of the world. His desire is that our **FRUIT SHOULD REMAIN** (verse 16). The truth is: *not all fruits keep.* Lasting fruit is the product of a branch that wholly abides in Jesus the Vine, Who said, "*Without Me you can do nothing*" (verse 5).

The Father is most glorified by fruit that lasts, which requires the three virtues of diligence, patience and the willingness to be hated for His name's sake. Fruit that remains is very rare in the Church today, because we have become satisfied with "results" that are little more than temporary "shots in the arm." We will explain the difference between results and fruit in the next chapter.

What Is Clear?

If I want my fruit as a branch to *multiply and last* for God's glory, I must abide in the Vine and gratefully receive the Vinedresser's pruning!

 1 Timothy 2:2 names a very crucial intercessory prayer petition, that we are to pray specifically *"for kings and all who are in authority."* Put simply, the surest way to bring needed change or correction to our local, state or national government is through prayer. As important as it is to pay attention to politics and to exercise our right to vote, it is *far more important and effective* to exercise our responsibility to *pray* for our leaders!

Parents and Grandparents will find that prayer concerning a child's behavior is far more effective than any one disciplinary technique. Some behavioral problems (in both children and adults) can only be corrected by the power of God through powerful, persistent prayer.

It boils down to this: Abiding in Jesus the True Vine, and abiding in prayer to our Heavenly Father the Vinedresser, are the two great secrets to fruitfulness.

Romans 12:6 names "Prophecy" as a Spiritual Gift. Take care that you do not see this word and automatically think of "explaining or predicting the future." The role of this Gift is to reveal the Father's heart by explaining what He is doing or the direction He is leading. On various occasions the person who has this gift may explain what it is that God wants "corrected," may bring to light things that have been hidden from or overlooked by others, and may help the church by explaining the "big picture."

If you have the Spiritual Gift of Prophecy you probably are supernaturally attracted to ministries like: Outreach ministry, Jail and prison ministry, Counseling, Long-range planning, Church council, and Personnel committees or teams.

What Motivates God?

Usually Does
Too Often Does Not

PERSONAL REPORT CARD

____ ____ Displays the fruit of the Spirit in daily living

____ ____ Wins people to Jesus

____ ____ Understands when and why the Father brings correction

____ ____ Helps to restore relationships

FAMILY REPORT CARD

____ ____ Raises children in the training and admonition of the Lord

____ ____ Bible study and teaching occurs in the home

____ ____ Rejects worldly training for spiritual training

____ ____ Creates an atmosphere in the home that encourages worship

CHURCH REPORT CARD

____ ____ Membership consists of people seeking unity and truth

____ ____ Pastor functions in a manner that is non-controlling

____ ____ Members refrain from trying to be "in charge"

____ ____ Members compassionately hold one another accountable

Notes On "Correcting from The Father's Heart"

_____

_____

_____

_____

_____

_____

_____

_____

_____

_____

_____

_____

_____

_____

_____

_____

_____

_____

Journal Of Turning Points

"To him who knows to do good and does not do it, to him it is sin." *(James 4:17)*

DATE | COMMITMENT

_____

_____

_____

_____

_____

_____

_____

"Men stumble over the truth from time to time, but most pick themselves up and hurry off as if nothing happened."

- Sir Winston Churchill

Chapter Three

Teaching from The Father's Heart

"Behold, God is exalted by His power; Who teaches like Him?"

- Job 36:22

Teaching is helping another to learn through the use of mental or physical activities, such as studying, thinking, reasoning, imagining, feeling, listening, talking, discussing, reading, writing and drawing. Various types of learning call for different kinds of activities.

God surpasses all other teachers as a teacher of men. Human instructors attempt to teach others while lacking a perfect knowledge and understanding of their pupils, themselves, or their subject. And human teachers lack the Divine authority of the Father, whose instruction is always perfectly suited for the occasion – and for the pupil's capacity to receive (see John 16:12).

When it comes to relevance, the Father's teaching concerns only those subjects about which man must be absolutely certain. Through the work of the Holy Spirit, only God provides perfect, full understanding and illumination with His instruction. (We will discuss this below.) Therefore, with consideration of great teachers past, present and future – no person even comes close by comparison to the Father, the Son and the Holy Spirit.

Father and Son

"A wise son heeds his father's instruction" (Proverbs 13:1). Although the very earliest religious teaching came from the lips of the mother, in the Jewish family, the person responsible for providing an education for the children was the father. Take a moment right now and read Proverbs 2:1-6.

Clearly the Father has a strong desire to teach and train His children. The earthly relationship between father and son is comparable to the spiritual relationship between God and His people. Therefore, there are certain characteristics found in a wise son that are also present in the child of God.

First, this wisdom is marked by *humble submission* that is not as much obligatory as it is desired. It is a wisdom that understands that we do not do well when we evaluate ourselves, because we cannot see ourselves as others see us. Second, and related to the first, this wisdom requires being a *good listener* when the father speaks. The father speaks remembering experiences that the son has neither faced nor understood. Third, the wise son not only "*heeds*" the father's instruction, but also stands *eager to receive* it. This third characteristic is particularly pleasing to our heavenly Father, who desires that His children be receptive to His voice of *perfect* wisdom.

In Proverbs 1:8, 4:1, 6:20 and 13:1, children are urged to understand and obey the instruction given by their fathers. Hint: These passages should be shared with children at the proper teaching opportunity, not during a moment of scolding or punishment. Furthermore, the unbelieving, ungodly parent can hardly expect a wise, conscientious child to obey their instructions for long, because that child will soon detect error and the absence of divine wisdom.

Christian teaching in the home is not a one-time effort; consistent repetition is a must. Opportunities to teach come daily. Therefore it is imperative that parents, who want their children to turn out well, know, understand and obey God's Word themselves. Blessed is the child whose parents teach by *manifesting* the Father's heart!

Family and Church

We understand "church" to be the gathering of God's people into His household, thus becoming His "family." We also understand that the Father rules, owns and dwells within His house. The church is said to be the *"sons and daughters"* of God (2 Corinthians 6:16-18). Thirty times in the book of Acts alone, the church is addressed as brothers, or *"brethren,"* a status dependent upon the work of the Father in His Son, Jesus (Hebrews 2:10-18).

The recorded words of Jesus reveal a close-knit, family-type relationship regarding His followers. He called them His "little flock." His connection to them was as Vine and branch. He was God's temple and His disciples were stones in that temple. Jesus described Himself as the Father's Good Shepherd and described His followers as sheep.

Two passages of Scripture come to mind (Matthew 16:17-19 and Matthew 18:15-20) that indicate Jesus "anticipated" the Church and saw it as part of His purpose. Here are ten desires and expectations of Jesus regarding this "family," several of which are included in his prayer recorded in John Chapter 17:

- This family *believes* that Jesus came from God the Father.

- This family is *on mission* to share the Gospel and to make disciples.

- This family is determined and focused on *glorifying Him.*

- This family is *obedient* to the Father.

- This family is under the direction of the *Holy Spirit.*

- This family is *close and united.*

- This family is *sustained by* the Father.

- This family has the *joy* of Jesus.

- This family not only knows "about" Jesus but also *knows* Jesus.

- This family is known by their *love.*

Perhaps your Bible study class at church would consider taking up a collection to provide Bibles to people who do not own a copy of God's Holy Word. Pray about making that an on-going gift, rather than a one-time event.

What priority does the ministry of teaching have at your church? Clearly it was a priority for the mother congregation at Jerusalem. Acts 2:42 says, *"And they continued steadfastly in the apostles' doctrine..."* indicating that the hearers not only attended the meetings faithfully, but also practiced earnestly what was taught.

True discipleship is unlikely to occur if we rely on the preaching alone, no matter how dynamic the preacher. Examine the spiritual growth and maturity of the saints at your church and determine if additional Bible teaching opportunities should be implemented.

Christians are to teach the observance of *"all things"* that Jesus commanded and taught (Matthew 28:20). This is a tall order for the Church, for our Lord gave instruction not only about doctrine and a variety of personal issues, but also about relationships – to ourselves, to one another and to Himself. Whether through the means of sermons, books, counseling, Bible study or discussion groups, the Church has a great responsibility and opportunity to teach from the Father's heart.

The Father Teaching through His Son

It was Jesus' desire not only to have disciples, but to have disciples who were teachable – most especially about how to make disciples of others. A true disciple may know little to begin with, but he will not be satisfied to remain in the dark.

Clearly, Jesus placed a high priority on that part of His work that consisted of teaching. He spoke to the importance of His teaching during the intercessory prayer recorded in John Chapter 17: *"I have manifested Your name* to the men whom You have given Me out of the world" (verse 6). His teaching of the disciples insured that His influence on the world and the advance of the kingdom would be permanent.

Jesus' principle *method* of teaching was "show and tell." He would do something, and then explain it. The disciples' principle method of learning, then, was "seeing and hearing." They would watch Jesus, and then receive a revealing explanation from Him. The results of this teaching process not only educated the twelve, but also gave them credibility when speaking to others about the Lord, enabling them to testify, *"That which we have seen and heard we declare to you"* (1 John 1:3).

His classrooms included the Temple, a mountainside, and a lakeside. He had no visuals, amplification or electronic aids. Yet the Father is still teaching through His Son, and we do well to pause and pray: *"Teach me Your way, O Lord; I will walk in Your truth; unite my heart to fear Your name"* (Psalm 86:11).

His amazed listeners declared, *"Where did this man get these things?"* (Mark 6:2), and, *"No man ever spoke like this man!"* (John 7:46). Almighty God said, *"This is My beloved Son. Hear Him!"* (Luke 9:35). What testimony could be more convincing than this, regarding *our* need – to both understand and obey Jesus' teaching?

As we said earlier, one of the ways that the Father reveals His heart is through the words and example of His Son. Hebrews 1:1-2 explains, *"God, who at various times and in various ways spoke in time past to the fathers by the prophets, has in these last days spoken to us by His Son."*

From the revealing and essential lessons of the Master recorded in John Chapter 15, we draw the following conclusions about some very important subjects to the mature believer:

What Motivates God?

1. Regarding Who We Are and Why We are Here
   We are living branches connected to the living
   Vine, and we are here to bear fruit. We were saved
   in order that *others* could eat the fruit we bear, in
   whatever location He has placed us. This is our
   "spiritual job description." I have read a lot of
   books by Christian authors over the years and seen
   numerous statements that suggest why you and
   I exist. *Jesus* said we are branches and we exist to
   bear fruit.

2. Regarding the Difference between Results and Fruit
   Results are religious substitutes for fruit, and are
   man's creation. Results may even include impres-
   sive statistics that man rationalizes to be fruit. Results are the number of vehicles we bring into the
   parking lot. Fruit is the number of souls we bring
   into (and then disciple for) the kingdom. Results
   cannot produce fruit, because results do not contain the *seed* that produces *more* fruit.

3. Regarding the Difference between Fruit and Fruit
   that Remains
   Fruit that remains and brings the highest honor to
   the Father is permanent growth, not a mere spurt,
   such as the short-lived fruit we often see today (see
   Matthew 13:20-21; John 6:66). Notice from John
   15:16 the role of the power of God through *prayer*
   in producing fruit that remains. Only by costly,
   prevailing, sustained prayer will fruit of this quality
   arrive and remain!

The Father Teaching through His Word (2 Timothy 3:16)

*"All Scripture is given by inspiration of God, and is profitable
for doctrine..."* in addition to three other effects (reproof,
correction and instruction in righteousness). The word

"doctrine" here refers to "teaching" on two levels. First, the Bible is profitable for teaching on a general level, meaning a description of how to make progress and how to mature in the Christian faith. Second, and in the context of the previous verse 15, Scripture is profitable for teaching "*how to make you wise for salvation through faith which is in Christ Jesus.*" This truth has value worth special attention.

The *only* place where we can be taught the *whole truth* about *the most important information needed by all mankind* – is in the Word of God. I can't speak for you, but I think this is an awesome fact! Any other non-fiction book, about any subject, by any author, brings no absolute assurance to the reader regarding truth.

Paul, writing to the church at Thessalonica, expressed these words of gratitude: "*For this reason we also thank God without ceasing, because when you received the word of God which you heard from us, you welcomed it not as the word of men, but as it is in truth, the word of God, which also effectively works in you who believe*" (1 Thessalonians 2:13). Let all Bible preachers and teachers take note: (1) So much depends on the heart of men who deliver and explain God's Word! (2) The Word of God, by its *own* nature and by its *own* power, produces this type of receptivity and acceptance by men; it is not the effect of man's personality or technique.

You will agree with me that life's most important decision is whether or not to trust Jesus Christ for salvation. But what if we had to launch a worldwide search or conduct a life-long study, to discover what we have to do to be reconciled to the Father? What if each of us was just "on his own" to try and figure everything out?

Jesus prayed to His Father, "*Sanctify them by Your truth. Your word is truth*" (John 17:17). Hold your Bible in your hand for a moment. There, right there in your hand, is *reality and truth*! The only infallible source of truth! That's what the Father is saying to you about His Word!

What Motivates God?

The following quotes of reflection come from Edward Irving's *Orations for the Oracles of God*: "Who feels the sublime dignity there is in a saying fresh descended from the porch of heaven? Who feels the awful weight there is in the least iota that hath dropped from the lips of God? Who feels the thrilling fear or trembling hope there is in words whereon the eternal destinies of himself do hang? Who feels the tide of gratitude swelling within his breast, for redemption and salvation...?"

My thoughts right now are about the many thousands of people who do not even own a Bible – who cannot do, if they wanted to, what you, dear reader, may have just done, and hold God's Word in their hands. Recently in Haiti, I saw the facial expressions of people receiving the gift of their first Bible. Their countenance revealed that they understood that something *holy* was being placed in their hands.

Oh, if we in America had that *awe* regarding God and His Word! Intercessors who pray with a kingdom-focus are pleading for this type of awakening in the United States and throughout the world. Will you join them?

Jesus the Student

It seems likely that Jesus knew three languages. *Aramaic* was the language of His country, although He probably did not read the Scriptures in this language. You will remember Him speaking in Aramaic when He raised the daughter of Jairus, saying, "*Talitha, cumi*" (Mark 5:41). Christ was brought up in Galilee where *Greek* was the language spoken, and a version of the Old Testament written in Greek known as the Septuagint was likely read by Him.

A third language Jesus probably knew is *Hebrew*, although, before Christ's time, this language had ceased to be the spoken language of Israel. The Old Testament was written in Hebrew but had degenerated into Aramaic. Yet scholars have observed that there were occasions when Jesus was quoting the Old Testament and spoke the reference in Hebrew rather than Greek. Also worth noting is the fact that He was asked to read the Hebrew of the Old Testament Scriptures in the synagogue of Nazareth.

Amazingly, our Lord probably did not possess a Bible of His own. For one thing, in those days it was very expensive to own a copy of the Scriptures, and the bulkiness of the scrolls kept them from being portable even for those who could afford them. There may have been a few scrolls available in His home, but more than likely Jesus gained His knowledge of the Scriptures during His many visits to the Synagogue.

Yet He was definitely a Bible student! Throughout the Gospels we hear Jesus quoting Scripture. Specific references to verses, as well as references to Old Testament events and personalities, rose from His heart until spoken at the perfect time and place. Personally, I find the Old Testament to be unusually special and comforting, just to think on the fact that I am reading the very words that Jesus studied and took to heart!

In what specific ways do we notice the Scriptures being a blessing and use to Jesus? First, He used the Scriptures for *inspiration*. As a Man rejected, persecuted and misunderstood, Jesus found companionship with men such as Moses and Elias and others by reading the Old Testament.

Second, Jesus received *guidance and understanding* through His study and knowledge of the Scriptures. He studied the prophecies of the Old Testament about Himself. Over and over it is said that our Lord did one thing or another – that a certain prophecy might be fulfilled.

Third, the Savior used His knowledge of the Scriptures as a *defense* against temptation and the assaults of wicked men. When tempted by the devil in the wilderness, Jesus answered each attack with, "*It is written.*" On numerous occasions when His enemies tried to confuse or trick Him, He repelled their attacks with answers drawn from the Scriptures.

The Father Teaching and Illuminating through His Spirit

The Holy Spirit illumines the minds and opens the hearts of the readers of God's Word to receive God's truth. Matthew 22:29 records Jesus saying to the Sadducees of His day, that their teachings contained errors that caused them to be *"Mistaken, not knowing the Scriptures nor the power of God."*

Psalm 36:9 says, *"In Your light we see light."* The Father does not merely "inform our minds." Through the Holy Spirit's enlightenment, He allows us to recognize such things as *"the beauty of holiness"* (Psalm 96:9). He brings certainty to our souls (see 2 Timothy 1:12).

Billy Graham has urged people to study the Scriptures – even when they may not fully understand what they are reading! This is because the very act of reading the inspired Word of God gives the Holy Spirit the opportunity to enlighten us. Paul explains in 1 Corinthians 2:10 that the things the Father has prepared for those who love Him are *"revealed... through His Spirit."*

John 14:26 names two magnificent ways in which the Holy Spirit works: by bringing to memory the words of Jesus, and by teaching all things. Here is a brief explanation of each function.

First, there are occasions, whether for our own good or in service to Him, when we need to remember what Jesus said. Perhaps when we were tempted, or when we were attempting to lead someone to Jesus, we suddenly remembered the very Scripture we needed – even when we had not looked at that particular verse for quite some time. It was the Holy Spirit at work!

Second, 1 John 2:27 says, *"You do not need that anyone teach you."* Sadly, I have heard ministers who were lacking in education (many of whom had simply not had the wherewithal or opportunity to receive it) quote this verse as proof that higher learning is unnecessary. They miss the point, which is that the Father's teaching through the Holy Spirit to those who *"abide in Him,"* surpasses that of all other teachers.

People who say that they doubt their ability to memorize Scripture forget that it is not about their ability; it is about their *desire*. The Holy Spirit will honor that desire by coming to their aid. I am also concerned for people who hurry to the bookstore or to the Internet as soon as they learn that a particular author's latest book is available. I do not want people to react that way to my books. The only book worth "hurrying" to, is the Word of God.

As an author and teacher, I am still learning. I realize that the direct teaching of the Holy Spirit is desirable above all else. Although the Holy Spirit may have taught me something as recently as yesterday, when I engage the Word of God today, I must once again desire the power and teaching of the Holy Spirit. All the Greek and Hebrew studies, all the study required to obtain all the degrees that exist, all the books in the largest theological libraries – while they have their place – must be illuminated by the Spirit's teaching for one to know perfect truth.

To those of you who teach a Bible study group, I urge you to connect every lesson you teach to *Jesus* – whether you are teaching topically or from any book in the Bible. Teach out of your knowledge of the Father's heart. Be sure to answer these two questions every time you teach: (1) WHY is this lesson *valuable* to a Christian? And (2) HOW can you *apply* this lesson from day-to-day? A teacher in the Church of Jesus Christ has done little of any consequence until his teaching has resulted in *action* taken by the pupil.

What Motivates God?

How should all believers respond to the Bible's teaching concerning the Father's *holiness*? Since God is holy and His teachings are holy, then you should desire to be conformed to Him *"because it is written, 'Be holy, for I am holy'"* (1 Peter 1:16). This is not out of reach, because God did not say, "Be *as* holy as I am." Your behavior can and should be holy. 1 Peter 1:15 says, *"But as He who called you is holy, you also be holy in all your conduct."*

How should you respond to the Bible's teaching concerning the Father's *infinite knowledge*? You should pray to "Him who sees me" (Genesis 16:13) when you are tempted to sin. How should you respond to the Bible's teaching concerning the Father's *infinite wisdom*? Imagine being advised by a consulting firm with perfect, infinite wisdom! The management of your life, if your level of faith will allow it, can be in the hands of One who knows everything!

The best guide for your life is to search the Scriptures, as Jesus did, seeing it as *the* chart for your time on earth. If we will submit to this discipline, one day we will be able to say as He did, *"This has been done that the Scripture might be fulfilled."* (See John 13:18 as one of many examples.)

What Is Clear?

I must not only have knowledge of spiritual things, but I must also have *spiritual* knowledge of spiritual things!

When your church holds special conferences and meetings, I expect that there are times of prayer "prior to," and even "during" the event. But are we ever encouraged or mobilized to pray "after" the event?

John Hyde (known as "Praying Hyde") believed with M'Cheyne Paterson, that it is immediately AFTER the seed is sown that the birds come and devour the seed, *"THEN the devil comes and takes away the word out of their hearts"* (Luke 8:12, capitalization added by the author). The time for very earnest, definite prayer is IMMEDIATELY AFTER the service or meeting, for the desire of the Father's heart is for fruit that REMAINS. After the meeting, then, is the time when the prayer room should be full with intercessors pleading that the seeds would not be devoured and that fruit from the meeting would be permanent.

The teaching ministry of Ministerial staff, Sunday School teachers and Bible study leaders should be prayed for regularly. Much is at stake!

 Believers who have the Spiritual Gift of Teaching (Romans 12:7) have the role of explaining the Bible in such a way that the spiritual health and ministries of the church are strengthened. They enjoy time alone for study, research and prayer. It is important to them that people actually *learn* something when they teach. Their teaching ministry could manifest through radio, television, music, writing, preaching, Bible teaching, drama or puppet ministry.

If you have the Spiritual Gift of Teaching, you are supernaturally motivated to take part in or to establish such ministries as: Vacation Bible School, Tutoring, English as a Second Language (ESL), Businessmen's luncheon, Nursing home ministry, or New members class teacher.

What Motivates God?

Usually Does *Too Often Does Not*

PERSONAL REPORT CARD

____ ____ Listens humbly to his/her earthly father (if present)

____ ____ Understands and fulfills his/her role in the family

____ ____ Understands and fulfills his/her role in the church family

____ ____ Regularly memorizes Scripture

FAMILY REPORT CARD

____ ____ Children are taught and reminded concerning who they are and why they are here

____ ____ Family members assemble in the home to read God's Word

____ ____ Bible verses and stories are applied to life circumstances

____ ____ Each family member owns a copy of God's Word

CHURCH REPORT CARD

____ ____ Leadership places a high value on the teaching of God's Word

____ ____ Members speak to and treat one another like a close family

____ ____ Visitors detect a family atmosphere and are treated in a special way

____ ____ Members are encouraged to read their Bibles and to bring their Bibles to church

Notes On "Teaching from The Father's Heart"

_____

_____

_____

_____

_____

_____

_____

_____

_____

_____

_____

_____

_____

_____

_____

_____

_____

_____

_____

Journal Of Turning Points

*"To him who knows to do good and does not do it,
to him it is sin." (James 4:17)*

DATE | COMMITMENT

_____

_____

_____

_____

_____

_____

"The difficulty lies, not in the new ideas, but in escaping from the old ones."

- John Maynard Keynes

Chapter Four

Listening from The Father's Heart

"He who planted the ear, shall He not hear?"

- Psalm 94:9

Whatever abilities are found in man are most assuredly found in the One who *made* man, and the ability to both hear and listen is no exception. That no noise has ever been made on earth that He did not hear is amazing enough, but to realize that He actually listens when we speak to Him in feeble prayer is truly amazing!

The Father listens to our private, personal prayers. The Father listens to our devotional prayers of praise and worship. The Father listens to our corporate prayers made in harmony with one another and the Holy Spirit.

Read all the books you can about prayer, attend all the conferences you can about prayer – but unless you can be certain that the Father *listens* to prayer, all talking and teaching about prayer is useless.

The Father Listening to His Children

"O You who hear prayer," declares David (Psalm 65:2). Calvin said, "God can no more divest himself of his attribute of hearing prayer than of being." To be *certain* that He hears, brings such comfort! Indeed He *must* hear, because He is faithful to His promises.

Prayer, at its best, is not simply about petitions for good weather, successful surgeries and improved circumstances. Those prayers seek the Father's "hand." True prayer is about an *intimate relationship*, which requires seeking His *"face"* (2 Chronicles 7:14). It is about two friends sharing their hearts.

What Motivates God?

There are hindrances to the Father hearing His children pray. For example, Psalm 66:18 says, "*If I regard iniquity in my heart, the Lord will not hear.*" (The most difficult sins to repent of are not the ones we've already committed, but the ones we *intend* to commit!) 1 Peter 3:12 says, "*For the eyes of the Lord are on the righteous, and His ears are open to their prayers.*"

Describing the attribute of the Father's "goodness," A. W. Tozer has written, "He hears prayer because He is good, and for no other reason." Seeing and fulfilling our needs is one of the roles of the Vinedresser. As we abide in Jesus the Vine, we are delighted in Him, and the Vinedresser listens to and answers our prayers. Psalm 37:4 says, "*Delight yourself also in the Lord, and He shall give you the desires of your heart.*" The Father wants communion with us. He wants to hear our prayers and give good gifts to His children.

Isaiah 65:24 says, "*It shall come to pass that before they call, I will answer; and while they are still speaking, I will hear.*" In fact, "*Your Father knows the things you have need of before you ask Him*" (Matthew 6:8). People still ask, in reaction to these verses, "Then why bother to pray?" That question reveals the lack of understanding that the true purpose of and reason for prayer is not about the request; it's about the relationship. Our very requests alone acknowledge that we are dependent on and need *Him*.

David said, "*In my distress I called upon the Lord, and cried out to my God; He heard my voice from His temple, and my cry entered His ears*" (2 Samuel 22:7). The Father desires us to seek Him through prayer. "*Then you will call upon Me and go and pray to Me, and I will listen to you*" (Jeremiah 29:12).

Matthew 7:9-11 says, "*Or what man is there among you who, if his son asks for bread, will give him a stone? Or if he asks for a fish, will he give him a serpent? If you then, being evil, know how to give good gifts to your children, how much more will your Father who is in heaven give good things to those who ask Him!*" Jesus is assuring us that our Heavenly Father is listening to and providing good things for us much more sufficiently than a sinful, earthly father can.

Living as a child of God, being led by the Spirit of God (Romans 8:14), we pray and are heard as a child. The Father's heart is for His children to trust Him as their provider for all things, living their whole lives in His presence and love. When we begin our prayers with the words, "Our Father," we should pause for a moment to realize that God, in His infinite love, patience and wisdom, is tenderly listening.

The Father Listening to His Son

There are at least nineteen occasions in the Gospels when Jesus is praying. But why would God need to listen to God? The answer is that Jesus was not half a man and half a God, but completely man and completely God. The Father spoke with His Son and Jesus listened; Christ prayed and the Father listened because of a *relationship* - between a perfect Man dependent upon His perfect Father.

Jesus did everything with total dependence on the Father. His works (John 5:36) and His words (John 14:24) came from the Father. How amazing! Jesus depended on prayer!

What a tender illustration of this dependency is provided in Mark 14:32-42 as we are permitted to hear Jesus' prayer in the Garden. Needing the ear of the only One who could possibly understand His feelings, Jesus knew without a doubt that the Father would listen lovingly to His Son.

Children Listening to Each Other

It has been said that there are three different kinds of speech: words that are spoken, words that are intentionally held back, and words that must remain in the depths of one's soul. Needy people do not always tell us the whole story, which means "reading between the lines" must be done carefully with discernment. When a needy Christian opens his mouth and speaks (particularly about himself), his spirit also speaks, giving the Spirit-filled Christian listener the opportunity to "touch" his spirit and minister supernaturally.

A Christian should listen to another person and hear not only what is spoken aloud, but also hear, with the discernment by the Spirit, what is *not* said. What I have just written is easier said than done. For when needy people speak to us, unless we are disciplined and Spirit-led, we will fail to recognize our ministry opportunity.

One risk of listening well is that we may hear something that could move us out of our own comfort zone made up of old ideas and old behavior. Listening is always a learning opportunity.

The tendency of the fleshly listener is to draw premature conclusions, or to wait for the opportunity to break in on the speaker in order to say something supposedly important. Referring to how poorly we listen to one another, Rebecca West says: "There is no such thing as conversation. It is an illusion. There are intersecting monologues. That is all."

West exaggerates, but my observation is that *few* Christians are good listeners. Many of us, whether as friends, parents or spouses, are prone toward advice-giving or just excessive talking. Ah, but when we listen well, we tell someone, "I care," *without speaking a word!* And we listen best to one another when we listen with the interest and compassion of the Father's heart.

Children Listening to the Father

Fifteen times in the New Testament Jesus is quoted saying, *"He who has ears to hear, let him hear!"* Listening to the Father must become vital to us. But *how* will we listen, and through what *means* does He speak?

While it is true that the "primary" way that we hear the Father's voice is from reading and hearing Scripture, we also learn to recognize His voice and to listen to Him as we abide in Him. Abiding includes two-way communication.

> *I come to the garden alone,*
> *While the dew is still on the roses;*
> *And the voice I hear, falling on my ear,*
> *The Son of God discloses.*
> *And he walks with me, and he talks with me,*
> *And he tells me I am his own,*
> *And the joy we share as we tarry there,*
> *None other has ever known.*
>
> *- C. Austin Miles*

Listening to the Father (or "meditating") is one of the most neglected but important pieces of a believer's prayer life. It is what converts a one-way monologue into a two-way conversation. Unfortunately, we often would much rather tell God what we want Him to do, than to take the time necessary for "intentionally" listening for the Father to tell us *His* agenda and *His* heart.

The Psalmist uses the word, "Siach," (to pray, commune or meditate) with reference to prayer in Psalm 55:17: "*Evening and morning and at noon I will pray, and cry aloud, and He shall hear my voice,*" and the same word is used in Psalm 77:6 and in Psalm 119:15, 27 ("meditate"), in Job 7:11 ("complain"), in Psalm 69:12 ("speak"), in Isaiah 53:8 ("declare") and in Psalm 143:5 ("muse").

The first thing Jesus taught the disciples about prayer is that they must find a solitary place (Matthew 6:6). During my seminary days I became close friends with one of my professors, Dr. Clyde T. Francisco. I will always remember the occasion on which I entered his bedroom at home, and saw a worn out, oversized chair in the corner by a window. It was clearly the special place where he and the Father spoke and listened to one another. Just to see that special chair, having spent many hours listening to this man's marvelous teaching, was an inspiration to me.

Personally, I have used a variety of different rooms and places over the years where I have shut out the world and its distractions. Currently, because I am blessed to live near the Atlantic Ocean, my "favorite" place to intentionally listen to the Father is along the beach.

It is easy for me to feel childlike there, as I occasionally notice small children (and adults) with their little buckets and shovels. Looking out toward the vast ocean, I am quickly reminded of His greatness and my smallness. The visible beauty, the sounds, the smells, the feel, and the ocean breeze – all blend together for a very soothing and relaxing opportunity to deliberately be in the Father's presence and to listen for His voice. In that sanctuary, it is easy for me to feel the warmth and the light of His countenance.

Regardless of where my solitary place may be with the Father, I leave His presence with a childlike faith and confidence. "Be still," says God's Word, "and know that I am God" (Psalm 46:10).

Listening to God is a learned discipline. Establish an activity or location where you can intentionally hear God without interference.

Being still also enables us to hear the *convicting* voice of the Father through the Holy Spirit. Some believers play a game with conviction, telling the preacher after the church service, "You really stepped on my toes," only to continue to wink at the sin in their lives. The sincere believer, however, *desires* the conviction of the Holy Spirit and *acts* upon it – so that his heart will be pure and holy before the Father.

And so, my dear Brother or Sister: Go to the secret place often! "*Shut your door.*" Listen to the Father's heart!

The Still Small Voice

We should be open to the possibility of the Father speaking to us in whatever "manner" He chooses. Sometimes the Father, according to His sovereign will, opens and closes doors through the circumstances of life. At other times, He actually "addresses" us in various ways – perhaps the most significant of which is the "still small voice."

This phrase is found in the story of Elijah, specifically 1 Kings 19:12: "*And after the earthquake a fire, but the Lord was not in the fire; and after the fire a still small voice.*"

The Father was teaching Elijah the difference between His power and His presence, and the fact that He uses small things to open mighty doors. It is a voice of gentle silence, a gentle blowing; a secret voice speaking to the mind. This is why the devil attacks the mind – the place where God communicates. Only a *listening* man can hear the still small voice.

Do not confuse the still small voice with your "conscience." Consciences vary from person to person, primarily because the parenting varies that molds the conscience early in life. "Let your conscience be your guide" may be a popular principle held by many, but Paul warns that the conscience can be "*seared*" (1 Timothy 4:2) by sinful activity, and can be affected by the actions and teachings of others (1 Corinthians 10:28-29).

By contrast, the still small voice has no variance, and is *always* in agreement with the Word of God. This is the Father's gentle voice that will at times warn of danger, encourage you to overcome temptation, or bring a Scripture verse to mind at just the right moment. "*Your ears shall hear a word behind you, saying, 'This is the way, walk in it'*" (Isaiah 30:21).

Neither sermons nor circumstances convert men, but rather the message and influence of the still small voice of the Holy Spirit.

The Church Listening to The Spirit

One of many results of true revival and spiritual awakening is that listening to the Spirit of God becomes *vital* to the Church.

The Holy Spirit speaks! In 1 Timothy 4:1 we find these words, "*Now the Spirit expressly says...*" and seven times in the letter to the churches in Asia we find the statement, "*He who has an ear, let him hear what the Spirit says to the churches*" (Revelation 2:7, 11, 17; 29; 3:6, 13, 22).

"*The churches*" refers not only to individuals within each of the seven churches named, but also to all believers in all churches of all places and all times. There was serious need to demand attention to this letter, mainly due to its clear statements regarding the *dangers* facing these named churches and all churches to follow.

The fact that the Spirit is speaking – not only in a personal way with individual men (*He* who has an ear), but also in constant and personal communication with individual churches (what the Spirit says to the *churches*) – places a huge responsibility upon the body of Christ to make listening to the Spirit a priority!

For one thing, the Church needs to hear the Spirit speaking words of "warning" to the saints due to the continuous and dangerous spiritual warfare taking place. In his small but helpful book, *Destined For The Throne*, Paul Billheimer writes, "Prayer... is God's way of giving the Church 'on the job' training in overcoming the forces hostile to God. God designed the program of prayer as an 'apprenticeship' for eternal sovereignty with Christ. The prayer closet is the arena which produces the overcomer."

In addition, the Church needs to hear the Spirit speaking words of "evaluation" to believers so that we will measure our condition by *His* standards. We see this clearly in the description of the seven churches.

The Father "manifests" His heart through the church. Therefore, the church must first listen to the Father in order to know what it is He wishes to accomplish, and then ask the Father to do what He wants. The "ear" is the ear of the heart. Referring to His Son, the Father had told the disciples, *"Hear Him!"* (Matthew 17:5). Here we see the Son, referring to the Holy Spirit, saying, *"let him hear what the Spirit says."*

If leadership and believers are not intentionally listening to what the Spirit is saying to the church *you* attend, where is your church heading?

The Father always speaks with the desire to be heard effectively, which is demonstrated here through the literal translation: *"let him actually, effectively hear!"* We discern when the Spirit is speaking, being born of the Spirit and led by the Spirit. Divine truth enters by the ear, through an act of the will known as "hearkening." This act sometimes involves "inclining" the ear from all else. The Father wants His words to sink down into the ears of the Church in a *personal, impactful* manner. We should hear the Spirit's voice as we *"pray without ceasing"* (1 Thessalonians 5:17), individually and as a church.

The Spirit speaks primarily through Holy Scripture. But if the Bible becomes the *only* means through which church members attempt to listen to the Father, a concern develops: Are these believers preferring a "text only" or "sermon only" relationship, instead of an actual "personal" relationship with the living God? The Bible may *provide* the text that God wants your pastor to preach from this Sunday, but he should be *guided* to that text by the Spirit – as the result of time spent in intimate communion with the Father.

Yes, the Spirit may at times speak through teachers, books, friends, music or sermons. But if we are not alert, remembering to *"test all things"* (1 Thessalonians 5:21), then these messages can easily become substitutes (merely "encouragement," "challenge" or "advice") for the Spirit's true voice.

Inwardly, I cringe when people say curious things to me at the church doorway following a worship service, such as, "I *enjoyed* that sermon" or "You really gave me something to *think* about." I was not in the pulpit for their entertainment or for intellectual stimulation. Clearly, giving consideration to a text or listening to a sermon is far easier to manage than the requirements of an intimate personal relationship!

The "God Told Me To" Obsession

A particular phrase is sometimes used among both ministers and laity who take advantage of the fact that we can hear God in ways other than through His Word. Too often for the purpose of disguising the truth, believers will explain certain decisions or behavior by saying, "God told me to." The use of this statement can become an obsession with a person who discovers how easily this phrase can be "successfully" used to avoid providing a truthful explanation to (or even a response to a sincere test by) fellow believers.

Once someone says, "God told me to," the case is closed! How do you argue with *that*? You cannot "prove" that it is not so (unless there is a clear contradiction to the Word of God). Consequently, a person can use this phrase either as a defense mechanism to justify virtually any (usually, self-pleasing) behavior – or to try to appear "super spiritual."

While the matter of using this phrase insincerely is a matter regarding integrity (a subject that will be examined in Chapter Six), I mention it now in the context of listening to the Spirit, in order to make the following statement. On occasions when God *really does* tell you to do or say something, you don't need to "declare" that He did, for the purpose of establishing credibility. Just obey! Let it be to you as a fast; keep it private. People walking in the Spirit will discern by the Spirit whether or not your actions, your decisions or your words are from God - *without your having to tell them.*

Webster's Dictionary defines the French word, *"faux pas"* (FO-pa), as a "social blunder." Someone should write a (humorous?) book that names various faux pas committed by Christians. I'll contribute one to get the brave author started: The preacher steps to the pulpit and announces to the congregation, "God changed my sermon." If this is true, and God cannot make mistakes, I'm wondering to whom the preacher was listening when he received the *first* sermon that we fortunately missed – and how does he know he's got it right *this* time?

What an awesome, humbling responsibility we who preach and teach the Word of God have, to listen well to the Father's voice before we stand in front of people with needy hearts!

What Is Clear?

The Father is speaking every day about things that man needs to know, and I must make a deliberate effort to hear Him!

God's Spirit alone knows what is in God. John 16:13 and 1 Corinthians 2:11 give us an indication of how serious and necessary it is to hear the Father and the Son through the Spirit. It is through listening to the Spirit that we *"know"* and understand the things of God and that we are guided *"into all the truth."* The Spirit is supremely qualified for this task because He is, after all, the Spirit *of Truth*, whose special work was to inspire and whose continued work it is to quicken, illumine and interpret the Scriptures.

65

What Motivates God?

As we have made clear repeatedly, prayer is a relationship that involves both speaking *and* listening. All believers who know and love the Father are interested in knowing *"the things which God has prepared"* for them (1 Corinthians 2:9), specifically, His purposes and His plans for each of our lives.

Having seen and understood this, do you sense the Spirit of God guiding you to better develop the "listening" portion of your prayer life?

 The Spiritual Gift of Ministry or Serving (Romans 12:7) is held by believers whose role in the church is to identify unmet needs and then make use of available resources to meet those needs as soon as possible. These people do not mind being personally inconvenienced if they can meet someone else's need. It is not easy for them to say, "no," when they are asked to do something. Their energy to fulfill various needs seems to be unlimited.

Believers who have the Spiritual Gift of Ministry or Serving are motivated supernaturally to establish or take part in ministries such as: Handyman ministries, Audio/video tape ministry, Van/bus driver, Media library, Nursery, Sound system, Building/grounds, Hostess committee, Daycare worker, or Usher/greeter.

Usually Does

Too Often Does Not

PERSONAL REPORT CARD

_____ _____ Sees prayer as an intimate relationship

_____ _____ Practices prayer as a two-way conversation

_____ _____ Has a solitary place for intimate prayer time

_____ _____ Differentiates between the voice of conscience and the still small voice

FAMILY REPORT CARD

_____ _____ Avoids interrupting when a family member is speaking

_____ _____ Family discusses what God is saying to them, individually and as a group

_____ _____ Listens for God to speak to the family through various means at various times

_____ _____ Family members will stop almost any activity to pray when the Holy Spirit prompts

CHURCH REPORT CARD

_____ _____ Membership has a good understanding of the conditions that can displease God

_____ _____ Leadership communicates clearly what the Father wants to accomplish for His glory

_____ _____ Pastor feels that it is more important for the members to hear God than to hear his sermons

_____ _____ Time is spent listening to the Father _before_ ministry activity is introduced to the church

What Motivates God?

Notes On "Listening from The Father's Heart"

_____

_____

_____

_____

_____

_____

_____

_____

_____

_____

_____

_____

_____

_____

_____

_____

Journal Of Turning Points

"To him who knows to do good and does not do it, to him it is sin." (James 4:17)

DATE | COMMITMENT

_____

_____

_____

_____

_____

_____

_____

*"It never troubles the wolf
how many the sheep be."*

- Virgil

Chapter Five

Protecting from The Father's Heart

"My Father, who has given them to Me, is greater than all; and no one is able to snatch them out of My Father's hand."

- John 10:29

Notice in John 10:28-29 that Jesus does not say that He or the Father will pluck His sheep *from out of the grasp* of a foe; no, He says that no foe will be successful in grasping a sheep out of either His or the Father's hand to begin with!

Behind all that Jesus *does* for His sheep, is His Father. All that Jesus *has*, comes from His Father. The sheep are safeguarded from any possible foe by the greatness and the power of the Father, whether the wolf is Satan, demonic spirits or human enemies.

Our spiritual life is in danger from numerous foes. These forces of opposition are relentless, but they will have to confront the awesome and limitless power of the Father. The truth is, we have very little comprehension of the perils we face on a daily basis. Lest you think I exaggerate, why do you think the full power of heaven is engaged for our safety?

2 Samuel 22:31 says, *"He is a shield to all who trust in Him."* Not only does He "provide" protection – as the Shield, He *is* the protection. Verse 33 continues, *"God is my strength and power." "He is our help and our shield"* says Psalm 33:20, and Proverbs 30:5 repeats, *"He is a shield to those who put their trust in Him."*

After George Washington officially resigned as Commander-in-Chief, he sent a circular letter to the thirteen governors and State legislatures that contained this prayer: "I now make it my earnest prayer that God would have you and the State over which you preside in *His holy protection*...to do justice, to love mercy, and to demean ourselves with that charity, humility, and [peaceful] temper of the mind which were the characteristics of the Divine Author of our blessed religion, without an humble imitation of whose example in these things, we can never hope to be a happy nation." (italics added by the author)[1]

Notice George Washington's understanding of the need for God's "holy protection" over our country, and his explanation that if we don't imitate Jesus Christ, America won't be a happy nation! (I must have overlooked that prayer in my American History textbooks.)

Our Father is the Fortress into which we can flee to safety. His presence surrounds us. This means that, *if we trust in Him*, our enemies have to conquer Him before they can injure us!

The Shepherd and The Sheep

As we mentioned in the Introduction to this book, one of God's names is "Jehovah-Raah" (or "Jehovah Rohi") which means He is seen as One tending, leading, feeding and protecting His flock. Sheep have a poor sense of direction, with no means of protecting themselves. When they are attacked by wolves, all sheep can do is run around until they are killed. Therefore, sheep must be watched and protected constantly lest they stray or come under attack.

David, himself a shepherd, wrote, "*The Lord is my shepherd.*" (Psalm 23:1) He was referring to Jehovah, the Lord God of Israel, who, when incarnate said, "*I am the good shepherd*" (John 10:11). God is often called the "Shepherd" of His people in the Old Testament (Psalm 80:1; Ecclesiastes 12:11; Isaiah 40:11).

---

1   George Washington, *The Last Official Address of His Excellency George Washington to the Legislatures of the United States* (Hartford: Hudson and Goodwin, 1783), p. 12.

The Son and the Father are equally concerned about protecting the sheep for good reason; the Son because of the mission received from the Father, and the Father because of the mission given to the Son. What a comfort to be reminded that the Shepherd and the Owner are one!

Sheep need to be saved, but they also need to be *kept* once they are saved; they require guidance, care, nursing and deliverance. Thus the Shepherd has a double duty: He has to feed the flock, but He also has to protect it.

Angels Protecting and Watching

The Bible describes the Father using angels to protect His children from potential enemies (2 Kings 6:14-17) and to minister to them in times of danger (Psalm 91:11 and Acts 27:23-25).

Psalm 34:7 says, "*The angel of the Lord encamps all around those who fear Him, and delivers them.*" When Peter was in prison awaiting execution, God's Word describes how an angel assisted in a mighty deliverance (Acts 12:5-11).

We know that angels are interested spectators of our lives. Paul wrote in 1 Corinthians 4:9, "*For we have been made a spectacle to the world, both to angels and to men.*" Hebrews 1:14 says, "*Are they* ["angels," verse 13] *not all ministering spirits sent forth to minister for those who will inherit salvation?*"

Matthew 18:10 is a verse used by many to support the "guardian angel" notion that every believer has his own, personal angel assigned to watch over him. The verse says, "*Take heed that you do not despise one of these little ones, for I say to you that in heaven their angels always see the face of My Father who is in heaven.*" Respectable Bible scholars disagree on the interpretation of this verse, but the previously mentioned verses clearly indicate that angels are used by the Father as ministering spirits and, on occasions of His choosing, for special assignments.

Unfortunately, angels are not the only ones watching us.

Wolves

In Scripture, the word "wolf" may refer to a powerful, fierce, covetous man or to a group of men. The tribe of Benjamin was likened to "*a ravenous wolf*" (Genesis 49:27). Jeremiah 5:6 describes Judah's enemy as "*a wolf of the deserts.*" Ezekiel 22:27 compares Israel's princes to "*wolves tearing the prey, to shed blood, to destroy people, and to get dishonest gain.*"

Wolves in the New Testament may refer to seducers and authors of wicked doctrine. Jesus repeatedly likened false prophets and false teachers to wolves. He applied the term to the critics and opponents of the early apostles (Matthew 10:16; Luke 10:3). Matthew 7:15 refers to false prophets as "*ravenous*" wolves, and Acts 20:29 speaks of "*savage*" wolves that will enter the church. Paul spoke of hypocritical, false teachers in Galatians 2:4 who "*came in by stealth,*" and similar warnings are found in the Epistles of Peter and John.

The wolf hunts singly, in pairs, or in packs. So cruel and devouring is the wolf that he kills not only what would satisfy his appetite, but the whole flock, if left alone. Wolves are strong, cruel, ravenous beasts.

What Does Sheep's Clothing Look Like?

Jesus warned, "*Beware of false prophets, who come to you in sheep's clothing, but inwardly they are ravenous wolves. You will know them by their fruits*" (Matthew 7:15-16). As we consider the protecting desire of the Father's heart, let's spend some time with these verses.

What are some characteristics of a false prophet or a false teacher?

- Says, "Thus says the Lord," when He did not; Says "God did not say this," when He did – all the while claiming to be moved by God.

- His teaching may be either "completely" false, or only "partially" false (which is still false).

- His true nature will manifest sooner or later, sometimes through a lack of integrity (which we will discuss later in Chapter Six).

- His effect on the church is to rend and tear the functionality and spiritual life of the body, like the fangs of a wolf.

- He deliberately takes advantage of the Church's general ignorance of the Word of God, along with the general lack of spiritual discernment among believers.

- His immorality and evil deeds may eventually become known, yet people will overlook his sinful behavior – sometimes, because they want to continue enjoying the things they like about him; sometimes, because they have shown previous support for him and their pride becomes a factor.

- Part of his disguise is his good works and outward appearances that are (by design) out front for everyone to see, so that he will appear as a "good tree" (Matthew 7:17-18).

What are some examples of the "garments" of a false prophet or false teacher?

- Uses smooth, kind words
- Quotes Scripture
- Persuasive, often distinguished
- Friendly, personable

Perhaps you respond saying, "Some of my favorite Bible

teachers and preachers have these same characteristics!" Of course they do; thus, the warning regarding the wolf's disguise!

What is *our* duty, then, toward receiving the Father's protection from the ravenous wolves in our midst? Here are the Bible's specific instructions:

- *"Do not believe every spirit, but test the spirits, whether they are of God"* (1 John 4:1). In Bible times, metals and coins were constantly weighed and tested before being accepted. The Spirit that is of God will honor Christ, both incarnate and crucified. Any spirit that encourages us to focus on ourselves and not on Jesus, is not of God. This instruction is for *all* believers, not simply clergy, and there are occasions when we must help one another to apply these tests – for our own sakes and for the sake of the church.

- *"You will know them"* (Matthew 7:16, 20) by their *"fruits."* "Know" means literally, "recognize" or "fully know." "Fruits" are a reference to the *doctrines* the false prophet teaches. Jesus pointedly assures us with this promise that discernment *"will"* occur, even with allowance made for both new and immature Christians in the church.

- *"Beware"* (Matthew 7:15) that these people do, in fact, *"come to you."* Literally, "keep holding your mind from," "watch out for." When wolves among us deliberately pretend to be sheep, we understand the seriousness! *"Inwardly,"* is a reference to their real nature, which leads to the lie of their appearance (a necessity, if people would receive what they offer).

Protecting the Flock

Words of prophecy may come to (or from within) today's church through evangelists, teachers and through believers who have been given the Spiritual Gift of Prophecy (Romans 12:6), which may or may not include pastors. But pastors, leading as shepherds, must guard and protect the flock.

Protecting from the Father's heart means looking out for signs that wolves may be raiding or molesting the sheep. Sometimes wolves have to be hunted down or trapped before the flock can rest with peace. Wolves will often watch every movement the sheep make over a period of time before making a swift, sneak attack. If the shepherd is prepared and knows the way in which wolves operate, he can possibly save the sheep from being slaughtered.

God rebuked Israel's leaders, calling them predators rather than protectors. Rulers of Israel were devouring the flock for their own gain (Ezekiel Chapter 34). The Father's heart caused Him to reverse the evils of the leaders, rescue His sheep and give them rest so they would no longer be prey. Sadly, this scenario is still seen today. Too many men who have the title and influence of the shepherd, behave more like sheep who are being led by others.

W.A Criswell tells the following story in his book, *Criswell's Guidebook for Pastors*: "When Dr. George W. Truett was invited to be president of Baylor University, he declined with one of the most beautiful sentences I ever heard. He said, 'No, I cannot come, for I have sought and found the shepherd heart.'" If a pastor desires to have the heart of a protective shepherd, what course should he take?

Acts 20:28 provides direction. Here are some truths that emerge from this verse:

- *"Take heed"* to be clean and taught yourself, before you try to cleanse and teach others.

- The church is a precious, united "*flock*" that follows and depends on the shepherd.

- If your heart is not large enough to care for "*all the flock*," it is not big enough to shepherd any of the flock.

The Church needs a fence, a wall to protect it from the wild beasts. Leadership in the local church must function in the same way as a fence functions for the house, the garden or the vineyard. The need is critical in today's church to thoroughly teach and disciple the flock so that they will receive the understanding needed to stand firm. The reason "*the whole armor of God*" (Ephesians 6:11ff) "works," is that it is not "our" armor, but *God's* armor.

His Eye is On the Sparrow

There are the occasions when we *realize* that the Father is watching with His loving, protective eye. For example, we may sense His protection as we ask for safety during a severe weather event, for journeying mercies when we travel, for security for our military personnel, for safekeeping when we sense the presence of danger or evil, for safety when other nations threaten our own, or for escape from the pursuit of our enemies.

When Robert the Bruce, the famous emancipator of Scotland, was fleeing from his enemies, he sought refuge in a cave. Although his pursuers were hot on his trail, when they reached his hideout a spider had built a web over the mouth of the cave. His enemies concluded that he could not have entered without first destroying the web. Naturally, they presumed that he had fled elsewhere. No wonder Bruce prayed, "O God I thank Thee that in the tiny bowels of a spider You can place for me a shelter, and then send the spider in time to place it for my protection."

Entering various voodoo temples in Haiti to speak with and pray for six witchdoctors in 2010 and in 2011, I was keenly aware of the dangers involved. The presence of evil in those temples was unspeakable. But the knowledge of the Father's protection and the favor resulting from powerful intercessory prayer brought perfect peace to my heart and kept me from any harm whatsoever.

On one occasion, an evil spirit manifested when I placed my hand on the head of a voodoo priest and prayed for him. God's protection was strong and complete! The evil spirit was addressed in the name of Jesus, left the man, and no harm came to anyone.

One of the most overlooked times when the Father protects His children is when we are tempted. God does not protect us from the *experience* of temptation; we *will* be tempted by the devil every day. What He protects us from is the temptation becoming *too intense in degree* or *too long in duration* with regards to our ability to endure (1 Corinthians 10:13). We are much in need of this protection, for without it, we would lose battles with the enemy consistently.

This protection reveals the *seriousness* of sin and of temptation. So concerned is our heavenly Father toward His children when we are tempted, that He sends His Son to come running to our side! Hebrews 2:18 says, *"For in that He Himself has suffered, being tempted, He is able to aid those who are tempted."* The Greek word for "aid" in this verse, literally means "to run speedily, immediately to one's help." It is the very same meaning as a parent running toward the sound of a cry of distress from a child.

And then there are the occasions when the Father protects us and we *never know of it.* Charles E. Bayley put it this way: "An accident occurs and we have a seemingly miraculous deliverance. Immediately we see God's hand in it and praise Him, even telling others of His marvelous act of providence. It never occurs to us to thank Him for the times beyond number when we were spared even the accident."

What Motivates God?

Perhaps, like me, you have given thought to the number of times the Father may have kept you from experiences such as a car accident, a plane crash, a disease, or someone's intent to hurt you in some way. The possibilities of His protection on occasions when we were unaware are endless. The devil is constantly lurking, looking for opportunities to hinder or harm us. But the good news is that our all-powerful Father is constantly protecting!

A Salute and A Thought

Long before the Twin Towers collapsed, and after, true heroes have been hard at work throughout our country. They are America's firefighters, police officers, and emergency medical personnel – people known as "first responders." Like our military, they are willing to risk their lives to serve and protect us. I salute them.

Firefighters and paramedics were among the first to answer the call of duty on the morning of September 11, 2001. Some 343 of those who came to save and protect lives, lost their own. Later, it was determined that 60 of those fallen firefighters had been off duty that day.

Speaking about these brave men and women, President Bush pointed out that they did not live to know who had caused the destruction or why. And then the President spoke these words: "They only knew their duty. And that was to go in, to follow the faintest cry, to search for the trapped and hopeless, and to save those who could be saved."

When I recently read these words of President Bush, I had a thought. While the President's words were clearly and appropriately spoken with reference to the firefighters and paramedics responding to the World Trade Center tragedy, do they not also apply to the duty of the Church of Jesus Christ?

What Is Clear?

I need to be more and more *spiritually* alert on a daily basis regarding the need for spiritual protection over myself, my family and my church!

 As we have seen in this Chapter, there are numerous ways in which the Father protects His children. Due to the relentless attempts made by the devil to tempt, harm and even destroy us, we should pray regularly for God's protection – and give Him praise and thanks for the occasions *unknown* to us when He was our shield.

Asking in prayer for spiritual discernment is becoming more and more necessary as we progress through these last days. Pray for discernment to recognize the wolves, because they do not all appear as wolves. Ask the Father for an even deeper hunger for studying His Holy Word, for the better your knowledge of the truth, the better your ability to detect error.

The role of the person with the Spiritual Gift of Giving (Romans 12:8) is to contribute material or financial resources to the church with liberality and cheerfulness. This person is able to discern how to insure that God's servants are fortified and that His kingdom is furthered. When they learn that their gift has been an answer to prayer, it gives them great joy. This person often gives an "offering" beyond the tithe and has a burden to meet the needs of missionaries.

Believers who have been given the Spiritual Gift of Giving are often found participating in such ministries as: Benevolence ministry, Food closet, Media ministry, Crisis pregnancy, Missions, Long-range planning, Scholarships, Love offerings to special speakers, and Pastor/staff appreciation.

What Motivates God?

Usually Does Too Often Does Not

PERSONAL REPORT CARD

____ ____ Remembers to thank God for the unknown as well as the known times when He has provided protection

____ ____ Tests the spirits when receiving teaching

____ ____ Remembers when tempted, that Jesus comes running to aid

____ ____ Personally speaks a word of thanks to first responders

FAMILY REPORT CARD

____ ____ Asks for the Father's protection when departing on family trips

____ ____ Prays for daily protection over each member of the family

____ ____ Discusses how God provides the family with constant protection, both known and unknown

____ ____ Prays for God's protection over schools and teachers

CHURCH REPORT CARD

____ ____ Leadership not only feeds the flock, but also protects it

____ ____ Pastor displays the heart of a shepherd

____ ____ Leadership avoids showing favoritism

____ ____ Church remembers to recognize and honor veterans and first responders in special services

Notes On "Protecting from The Father's Heart"

_____

_____

_____

_____

_____

_____

_____

_____

_____

_____

_____

_____

_____

_____

_____

_____

_____

Journal Of Turning Points

"To him who knows to do good and does not do it, to him it is sin." (James 4:17)

DATE | COMMITMENT

_____

_____

_____

_____

_____

_____

_____

_____

"You can't handle the truth!"

Colonel Nathan R. Jessep, USMC,
from A Few Good Men *by Aaron Sorkin*

Chapter Six

Leading from The Father's Heart

The Father's Heart is to Lead with Patience

"They shall come with weeping, and with supplications I will lead them... for I am a Father to Israel."

- Jeremiah 31:9

Although Jeremiah knows of the people's rebellion, he rejoices that God's stubborn people will return to the Lord. As believers, as families and as churches we have been the prodigal son many times over.

A patient parent looks at the tantrums of a child going through the "terrible twos," and responds by consistently providing a calm environment where the child can learn the fact that things will not always go his way. God's love, especially toward the weaklings, is always the perfect parent's love.

Every sin you and I commit is as though we did it right in front of the very throne of God. We should be amazed that we suffer so little for our rebellion. How patiently He observes our depraved conduct and continues to love us even while we reject Him. I read Nahum 1:3, *"The Lord is slow to anger and great in power,"* and I can only respond by praying, "Thank you, thank you, thank you, for Your patient leadership!"

Yet, as we consider His patience, let us be careful to not presume upon His mercy. God's redemptive purpose is achieved through man's penitence. The Father will not be unjust to Himself. He shows mercy to those who are truly penitent. His love is both the most awful and the most blessed fact that the soul can know.

The Father's Heart is to Lead with Integrity

Lying. *"An abomination to the Lord"* (Proverbs 12:22). I recall a song written many years ago and recorded by B.B. King entitled, "Everybody Lies A Little." The lyrics contain a line that says, "Some people say that lying is wrong; it's alright with me if it saves your life or your home. Everybody lies a little, sometime." The song cleverly describes what is known as "situational ethics."

Situational ethics is a morality acknowledging that any act – including (in worst case scenarios) abortion, divorce, cover-up, and murder – *could* be right, depending upon the circumstances.

On the less serious side, for example, applying situational ethics makes it acceptable to temporarily "lie" to children about the existence of characters like Santa Claus, the Tooth Fairy, or the Easter Bunny – as long as the parent views the deceit as "harmless role playing" or as "keeping a tradition," rather than as flat-out lying. But what about when situational ethics is practiced in larger arenas outside the privacy of the home, and when it affects large numbers of people concerning more serious subjects?

On June 18, 1948, the United States government made a decision that many Americans are unaware of to this day. On that day, the National Security Council sanctioned a top-secret, covert-action directive known as "NSC 10/2" which the Central Intelligence Agency (CIA) interpreted as a license to do incredible things when the perceived purpose was *achieving U.S. interests and goals.* Diplomat George Kennan sponsored NSC 10/2. He was quoted later confessing that this directive was the greatest mistake he ever made. [2]

NSC 10/2 contained a doctrine known as "plausible de-

---

2   Peter Grose, *Gentleman Spy: The Life of Allen Dulles* (New York: Houghton Mifflin, 1994), p. 293. (Note: Sometime around 1955, NSC 10/2 was replaced by NSC 5412/2, but plausible deniability was retained and is still in effect today.)

niability." The CIA understands "plausible deniability" to provide the U.S. government with *permission to lie to anyone about anything* whenever it is felt necessary to cover up any trace of accountability. Thus the less explicit an order from the president, the better it is for CIA autonomy and plausible deniability. (A number of people who are aware of how our government implements plausible deniability have wondered if it "may" have been used to explain such matters as "UFO's" or the assassination of President John F. Kennedy.)

While I am writing this book, there is an investigation underway at Penn State University involving plausible deniability in the world of sports. In recent years, the Catholic Church has tragically illustrated the existence of plausible deniability involving homosexual activity. Ho hum, we say with a sigh. Life goes on.

Although nothing official exists in writing that gives license to the local church to behave in any manner it wishes for the purpose of achieving various interests and goals, any careful and discerning observer of today's church can see something similar to "plausible deniability" at work. We are observing an alarming number of churches and religious organizations doing all sorts of things, making all sorts of decisions, following all sorts of "leaders" – all the while providing explanation, justification and even cover-up for what they know full-well is blatant, un-Christ-like, unScriptural, sinful behavior – "whatever it takes" to protect the name or reputation of a particular minister, church, or organization.

Do the Ten Commandments apply to only "certain situations" that are "fitting?" Did God forget to say to Moses, "Tell them there are some *exceptions*, but they can probably figure it out?" When Jesus said, "If you love me, keep my commandments," did He fail to add the qualifier, "Unless love for someone else, or sound reasoning get in the way?"

What Motivates God?

I have not lost touch with the headaches and the heart-breaks of life. But at the risk of sounding like a legalist, I'm simply pleading with our spiritual leaders: Don't live and teach situational ethics and plausible deniability to the extent that *God's commandments* become a blur alongside principles, recipes and "guidelines for living!" Compromising integrity is a blatant rejection of the authority of Jesus Christ!

Humbly and honestly consider these examples of Plausible Deniability at work in the Church, and repent of any personal or corporate sin that the Holy Spirit reveals:

Believers and church members rationalize sinful and unbiblical behavior, while plausibly denying the available power of God to resist the devil; forgive others with the lips, while plausibly denying the responsibility to forgive with the heart; fail to treat fellow believers with love and respect, while plausibly denying the responsibility to behave like compassionate sibling members of the family of God; blame the government for taking prayer out of schools, while plausibly denying our failure to evangelize the unbelievers who make the objections; express displeasure by withholding or redirecting financial gifts to the church, while plausibly denying the command of Jesus to first go to the offender in private and follow subsequent steps if necessary.

Pastors and religious leaders use plausible deniability to disobey the Holy Spirit for fear of reaction or rejection by church members, while plausibly denying the promises of protection and provision from God; plagiarize sermons or justify selfish behavior – using phrases like "God told me to," while plausibly denying the responsibility of honesty and integrity; adopt attitudes of denial and defensiveness, while plausibly denying God's command to humble ourselves and repent; consider fellow ministers as competitors, while plausibly denying the effect disunity among ministers has upon the church and upon a lost world.

Why am I spending so much time discussing situational ethics and plausible deniability? Because leading with integrity from the Father's heart – most assuredly when doing *His* Work and when leading *His* church – requires a conviction that "the end does *not* justify the means."

Leaders with integrity carry the Father's presence into the lives of people. Many of us are doing the opposite, trying to carry people into the presence of the Father. A Godly leader must first come down from His presence to minister with anointing from above. That determination and commitment to bringing God's glory to the people will bring fruit that remains.

How Should the Church Lead in Today's World?

Here are some exhortations I humbly offer the Church:

- Understand that *reputation* and *character* are two different things
- Build a *church*, not a *crowd*
- Promote *holiness* over *happiness* (even if it means loneliness and rejection)
- Evaluate both your *methods* and your *motives* concerning finances
- Seek the *approval of God* over the *applause of men*
- Discern the *condition of the flock* rather than simply the *number of the sheep*
- Care more about your pastor's *spirituality* than his *personality*

The Early Church in the Book of Acts was full of issues and abuses, even though it was of divine origin. Yes, it was the house of God. But over time, man kept adding his own things and his own behavior to it, until it became difficult to recognize the Father's original intent. And today's Church is no freer than the Early Church from the danger of man-made defects.

Have you ever been part of a performance-driven church? What about a church that resembles an army, or a classroom, or a funeral home? God spoke to Israel and said, *"Cast away from you all the transgressions which you have committed, and get yourselves a new heart and a new spirit"* (Ezekiel 18:31). Why did they need a new heart? Because the original heart was worn out from striving, performing, lack of preventive care, and sin. In many ways, this fits the description of today's church.

Churches best resemble the Father's heart that understand and follow the father-family concept. While families need the ingredients of instruction and obedience to be effective, there are several other elements to consider. For example, when we think of God-honoring families, size doesn't matter. With consideration to size, a small family can honor God as well as a large one. Financially, a poor family can be God-honoring as well as a wealthy one.

The Father is more concerned with how we *function* as a family than He is about "more money" and "more people." His heart for the church is that we would function by displaying love, care, encouragement and affirmation toward one another. Because He is holy, He desires that we demonstrate integrity in all that we do.

One of the things Jesus Christ came to tell us is that God wants us to know Him as our Father. Knowing the Father intimately brings us to the place where we realize how the Church should lead in today's world.

First, the Church in today's world must learn to *lead like a good father*. The world in which we live is alienated and isolated. Churches are not understood by the world because the "world" has not been placed in a "family." 1 John 3:1 says, *"Behold what manner of love the Father has be-*

stowed on us, that we should be called children of God! The world does not know us, because it did not know Him." Did you notice the language of "family" in that verse?

If a father says to his child, "Do as I say, and not as I do," he may succeed in getting the child to obey, but he will also succeed in revealing that he is a hypocrite. If a father says to his child, "Children are to be seen, and not heard," he may succeed in getting his child to be quiet, but he will also succeed in raising a child that may develop low self-esteem. A good father leads with warmth, humility and sincerity that result in healthy children who bear fruit.

Second, the Church in today's world must learn to *lead as the instrument in the eternal purposes of God*, which are (1) to bring all things under the Lordship of Christ, (2) to restore all things to God's original plan, and (3) to bring under one head all things in Christ. A prime responsibility of the Church is to lead out in the task of preaching and teaching the Gospel that men may be reconciled to God.

What is "the Gospel?" I still remember the answer to that question as taught by my seminary evangelism professor, Dr. Lewis Drummond. He taught our class that the *Kerygma*, i.e. message proclaimed, has seven points - *all seven of which must be included*:

- Jesus Christ is the promised Messiah.
- The age has dawned: the Kingdom of God is with men.
- Jesus lived, taught, healed and ministered.
- Jesus died by crucifixion for the sins of all mankind.
- God raised Him on the third day.
- He is coming again.
- Forgiveness and the gift of the Holy Spirit comes to those who repent and believe.

What Motivates God?

The Bible says that when the Gospel is proclaimed, it should be proclaimed in its *fullness*. The Father is interested in the *whole* man; there is no biblical justification for separating a so-called "social gospel" from a "saving gospel."

Third, the Church in today's world must learn to *lead with the same initiatives that are taken by the Father*. Many churches today do not understand the relevance of asking the questions, "What is God currently doing?" or "What is God about to do?"

I do not think that you want to be part of a church that believes it is acceptable to follow a different agenda from God's agenda. Can you imagine the shock of learning that your church is actively doing things that are totally unrelated to what God is doing in your community or in the world? If there is even a chance that this is the case at your church *or* in your life, fall to your knees and ask the Father to reveal *His* initiatives, while there is yet time!

There may be some who will read this chapter and label me a "basher" of preachers and churches – perhaps because they resent having their sins exposed, can't discern my broken heart, or can't handle the truth. The truth is that the Church, even in its worst days, has been unconscious of (or unwilling to face) its own defects – until those defects are pointed out lovingly and with discernment by someone who has a burden to see biblical reform and awakening come to the institution for which Jesus gave His life. I am trying to write compassionately. Those who know me well, know that I deeply love pastors and the Church. We are all in this crisis *together*.

The need is urgent for clergy and church members to take initiatives born from humility and in agreement with the Father's activities. But how can we see what initiatives the Father is taking? We learn through our connection as a branch with the True Vine. Jesus said, *"The Son can do nothing of Himself, but what He sees the Father do; for what-*

ever He does, the Son also does in like manner. For the Father loves the Son, and shows Him all things that He Himself does" (John 5:19-20).

Another way that we learn God's initiatives is to call to Him in prayer. Jeremiah 33:3 says, *"Call to Me, and I will answer you, and show you great and mighty things, which you do not know."* This verse makes it clear that the Father has no desire to "hide" important things from us.

There will be plenty of readers who understand that what I am writing not only needs to be "said," but also needs prayerful consideration with the response of biblical repentance. Is the Father speaking to your heart at this moment? If He is, please put this book down, listen, and then respond to Him.

The "Father's Business" (Luke 2:49)

Bibles with red print are still popular today. There's just something special about identifying and reading the words that were spoken by our Lord Jesus. Therefore, Luke 2:49 arrests our attention because it contains the first recorded words of Jesus! Of all the words that Jesus the child and young adult must have spoken until age thirty, here we have before us the *only* words God says we *need* to know. I wonder why, but I rest with peace that for some reason it pleased the Father to be silent about it.

The mention of His Father's "house" was not a reference to the magnificent Temple structure. It was the higher meaning of the word, namely *an understanding of the mission*. On this occasion, Jesus the child was apparently so absorbed with the realization of Who He was and what He was to do, that the normal interests for a youngster were not on his mind. Jesus the adult would later show the same preoccupation on an occasion when the disciples urged Him to eat, by declaring, *"My food is to do the will of Him who sent Me, and to finish His work"* (John 4:34).

What Motivates God?

We are familiar with the context and the setting of this passage. I wish to call our attention, then, to the words, "My Father's business," as we continue our look at the subject of Leading from the Father's heart. Interestingly, Bible scholars agree that the Greek may be translated as either, "My Father's business" or, "My Father's house."

Either way, we can say with confidence that children who wish to honor, support and serve their father need to understand what their father wants to accomplish. What is it that Jesus understood at such an early age about the things pertaining to His Father?

- What Jesus was doing in the Temple is what He saw His Father doing (John 5:19): anything to promote the kingdom, anything to clarify truth, anything that will lead to the salvation of man.

- Active participation was appropriate behavior in His Father's house (vs. 46-47).

- "I *must* be," indicates that Jesus was beginning to understand the magnitude of His mission on earth (vs. 49).

- Obeying His earthly parents was part of His Father's business, too (vs. 51).

In addition:

- It was important to increase in wisdom and stature (vs. 52).

- It was important to be in favor with His Heavenly Father and with men (vs. 52).

> ## What Is Clear?
>
> Jesus based His ministry and method on what He saw The Father doing, and my church and I must do the same, leading with integrity like a good father!

 Church leaders, especially, should be remembering to pray Matthew 9:38, for *"the Lord of the harvest to send out laborers into His harvest."*

As we have seen, patience and integrity are much needed qualities in church leaders today. When we see people lacking in these areas, our first inclination should be to pray for them rather than criticize them.

What is the Holy Spirit revealing about how you "function" as a family? As a church family? Are there any indications that the "end" has been justifying the "means" in one or both families? Do some serious listening to the Father as you pray about this.

Romans 12:8 names *"he who leads"* as a Spiritual Gift. This person's role in the church is to organize and coordinate in such a way that the goals of the church are achieved with harmony. The church member with this Gift is able to visualize the "overall picture."

Examples of the kinds of ministries that are well-suited for the person with the Spiritual Gift of Leadership would include: Sunday school/Training Director, Outreach/Visitation Director, Nominating Committee, Ladies/Men's Group Director, Worship Leader, Food Closet Director, Long Range Planning Team member, Vacation Bible School Director, Church Council Member.

What Motivates God?

Usually Does
Too Often Does Not

PERSONAL REPORT CARD

_____ _____ Personal behavior exemplifies the Father's attributes

_____ _____ Shows patience with children and with fellow believers

_____ _____ Makes a strong effort to practice integrity in all circumstances

_____ _____ Seeks to recognize and follow initiatives the Father is taking

FAMILY REPORT CARD

_____ _____ Home feels safe and secure

_____ _____ Family members practice integrity inside and outside the home

_____ _____ Family regularly talks together about the Father's business

_____ _____ Family has discussed all seven points of the Kerygma

CHURCH REPORT CARD

_____ _____ Leadership practices openness and integrity in church affairs and business

_____ _____ Leadership shows boldness yet patience with the members while they grow

_____ _____ Church ministries represent the points of the Kerygma well

_____ _____ Church bases its witness to the community and to the world based on what God is doing

Notes On "Leading from The Father's Heart"

_____

_____

_____

_____

_____

_____

_____

_____

_____

_____

_____

_____

_____

_____

_____

_____

_____

_____

Journal Of Turning Points

"To him who knows to do good and does not do it, to him it is sin." (James 4:17)

DATE | COMMITMENT

_____

_____

_____

_____

_____

_____

_____

"When we forgive,
we walk in stride with God."

- Lewis B. Smedes

Chapter Seven

Forgiving from The Father's Heart

"Forgiving one another, even as God in Christ forgave you."

- Ephesians 4:32

This kind of forgiveness can only be offered genuinely and fully by a believer who has himself been the recipient of such quality forgiveness as came by the Cross. Paul is saying that those who have been forgiven so much, and at so great a cost, will forgive others in a certain way. This verse makes the truth clear, then, that the *manner and motive* with which we forgive others is important to the Father.

The word which Paul uses for "forgiveness" in this verse is *charizomai*. Its primary meaning is "to grant as a free gift," and so it is a suitable word to denote the forgiveness of a debt. Whether the person we are forgiving repents, makes amends, or asks for our forgiveness – makes no difference. Paul is speaking here of our duty and the manner in which we must forgive someone.

In what manner does the Father grant forgiveness? *Freely and abundantly!* Matthew 18:21-22 tells us that Peter was wondering one day just how many times he needed to forgive a brother who continues to sin against him. Jesus answered, "*I do not say to you, up to seven times, but up to seventy times seven.*"

There are two basic conditions that have to be met before the Father forgives. First, we must repent. If He does not require repentance, it would appear that God was either condoning sin or being indifferent to it. Second, we must be willing to forgive others – a requirement that connects to the genuineness of repentance.

As for the believer's motive for forgiving, the reason

we forgive is not to achieve inner peace for ourselves, or to clear our conscience. No, the *relationship* is the central focus. Jesus said we are to go to our brother, and if he will hear us, we have gained our brother. The one thing that makes us the Father's "children," and thus "brethren," is the fact that our sins are forgiven.

The fact that God forgave our sins "in connection with Christ" is what must compel us to forgive every man who in any way sins against us. After all, the Father's forgiveness "*in Christ*" was completely invested in incarnate involvement, crucified self-commitment and life-blood contact – with us! Since there is no cheap forgiveness in Christ, our forgiveness of others must also be of the highest quality.

His Forgiveness and Our Fear

Psalm 130:3-4 says, "*If You, Lord, should mark iniquities, O Lord, who could stand? But there is forgiveness with You, that You may be feared.*" If the Father's record keeping was all about condemnation and was acted upon, no one could maintain innocence at any level. Consequently, fear that is reverence is the result of having relationship with such a forgiving Father.

It has been said that these two verses contain the sum of all the Scriptures. In the third verse is the form of repentance, and in the fourth verse the mercies of the Lord; in the third iniquities, in the fourth forgiveness. In his commentary on verse four, Charles H. Spurgeon wrote: "It is grace which leads the way to a holy regard of God, and a fear of grieving Him."

John Bunyan found consolation in these two verses during one of his "grievous and dreadful" onslaughts of the devil. He felt blessed to realize that God noticed not only his sins, but also his tears and faith.

The Cross and Forgiveness

1 Peter 2:21 says, *"For to this you were called, because Christ also suffered for us, leaving us an example, that you should follow His steps."* The Father knew that an unforgiving world needed an example, a model for forgiveness and compassion. Revenge is one of the sweetest satisfactions to the natural heart. Throughout His life, Jesus had been revealing the Father. But now, at the Cross, it was time to make known the very highest in God.

The Father took our condition of being lost in sin so seriously, that He went to Calvary to substitute Himself for us, to pay the debt for us. This isn't an ugly example of scapegoating on God's part, where Jesus becomes the victim because of our sins. For the sake of justice, the guilt of one's sins cannot be transferred to a third party; it must be settled between the two parties involved. That is why we read in 2 Corinthians 5:19: *"God was in Christ reconciling the world to Himself."*

When I was a child playing games with my siblings, they used to accuse me of "making up your own rules." I was more than likely guilty as charged, if I thought I could gain an advantage over my older brothers and sister. But if we want to forgive as God in Christ has forgiven us, we cannot do so by making up our own rules. God's way with us must be our way with each other. Forgiveness is not fully complete until the broken relationship is mended.

Jesus' public ministry had opened with prayer (Luke 3:21), and at Calvary we see it closing with prayer. From the Cross Jesus prayed, *"Father, forgive them, for they do not know what they do"* (Luke 23:34). I will make two quick comments regarding this prayer.

First, Jesus had no previous occasion to make such a request of the Father, because Christ could *Himself* forgive others. But on the Cross, hanging there as our Representative, He was no longer in the place of *authority* where He could exercise His own Divine prerogatives, and therefore had to ask the Father to forgive them.

Second, when Jesus prayed, "They do not know what they do," He did not mean that His enemies were ignorant of the "fact" they were crucifying Him. Jesus meant that they did not understand the "enormity," the "meaning" of their crime, therefore: "They do not know *what* they do."

Oswald Chambers wrote, "It is shallow nonsense to say that God forgives us because He is love. The only ground on which God can forgive me is through the Cross of my Lord. Forgiveness, which is so easy for us to accept, cost the agony of Calvary. When once you realize all that it cost God to forgive you, you will be held as in a vice, constrained by the love of God."

Another topic to understand when we consider the Cross and forgiveness is the "completeness" of the Father's forgiveness. Most believers understand that all of the sins they committed *before* they trusted Christ as their Savior have been forgiven. But sometimes Christians have difficulty with believing that the sins they continue to commit – *after* they are saved – are also forgiven.

Praising God as I write these words, let me state clearly that *all* of our sins – past, present and future – are covered by the blood of Jesus! If you struggle with this truth, maybe answering this question will help: Were not *all* of your sins *future* sins when Jesus died on the Cross? Of course they were, because you were not even born when Jesus was crucified!

Forgiveness 101 in Psalm 51

David prayed, "*Hide Your face from my sins, and blot out all my iniquities*" (Psalm 51:9). In Scripture, as long as our sins are not forgiven, they are represented as standing before the "face" of God in order to accuse us. As the Father looks upon the ugliness of our sin, He sees the transgression of His law and this awakens His wrath and displeasure. To "hide" the face from anything means not to see it.

In the fourth verse of this Psalm, David confesses to the Father that he has committed sin *"in Your sight."* Jeremiah 2:22 says, *"For though you wash yourself with lye, and use much soap, yet your iniquity is marked before Me, says the Lord God."* And so it takes a wonderful act of God's free grace for a sinner to receive the blessed certainty that his sin is no longer before God's face.

When God no longer sees our sin in wrath, but instead looks upon us with mercy, only then can we rejoice with the assurance of His favor. This is why we plead the promise of God and the great power of the blood of Jesus. Only our precious Savior is in position to cover our sins and take them away from the Father's face.

Then David continues in the same verse, *"And blot out all my iniquities."* The blotting out of a person's iniquities is the first blessing that the Father brings to the sinner who wants to be saved. From the moment of that first blessing, the blotting out of his sins is continuous, perfect and complete. At this point his soul appears before God *"whiter than snow."*

Just about now, you may have to put this book down because you cannot see the print through your tears! Perhaps you have begun to sing Psalm 103:1: *"Bless the Lord, O my soul; and all that is within me, bless His holy name!"* Sin can be put away! Without this blessing of blotting out, there is no salvation. Only God can give it. He desires to give it. He continues to give it. Yes, the Son of God is still saving sinners. Believe in Jesus and you will not be ashamed.

Steps

The easy way out when we are hurt is to simply reject the relationship. Having been hurt, we can simply write the person off, saying, "I never liked him anyway! Who needs him?" This reaction eliminates the work of restoring a relationship. But only if you have no need for forgiveness yourself, should you dare taking this approach.

Forgiveness is love's revolution against the cruelties of life. It is not a skill that is mastered. True forgiveness is a process that takes time. When we genuinely forgive others, we take a series of steps.

Step One: Look upon this person as someone for whom Jesus died.

Regardless of what this person has said or done, he has worth in the sight of the Father. He is a person of value. Like you, he is a precious soul for whom Christ gave His life. Don't lose sight of that, for it is a fact.

Step Two: Look at your pain with the Father.

You have been wronged. Your heart has been hurt. But your heart, like everyone's, is deceitful and you cannot understand it. In order to understand what has happened through the eyes of the Father, you need help. Jeremiah 17:10 says, "*I, the Lord, search the heart, I test the mind.*" Listen to Him through His Word, so that you will receive Divine understanding and discernment that leads to healing.

Step Three: Look at forgetting and forgiving properly.

Forgetting is not the first step; it is the last step. Forgetting is the "result" of true forgiveness, not a means of getting there. If you try and work up some kind of "spiritual amnesia," you will only become frustrated. Remember: True forgiveness is rare because it is both difficult and costly. "I'll never forgive," said General James Oglethorpe to John Wesley. Wesley replied, "Then I hope, sir, you never sin!"

Step Four: Look at the future humbly and with compassion.

The past is history; nothing can alter the facts. The future is a different story. Making angry demands or threats concerning future behavior will only lead to heartache. We are human beings and we will all continue to disappoint and to show our weaknesses – even with the best of intentions. No matter how many promises of perfection you may receive, there is nothing you can do that will guarantee a painless future. How many "second chances" has the Father given *you*? Reread Luke 17:3-4.

Step Five: Look at a new relationship.

Now is the time to forget. Invite the person who hurt you back into your life. If they accept your invitation, a new and healed relationship can emerge. If the person will not come back, you have to be healed alone. Relationships matter to the Father, and you have honored Him by taking these steps and by doing your part.

"Alright," you respond, "but you don't understand *my* situation."

What About the Really Difficult Cases?

There are some challenging circumstances and people that can exist, when we try to forgive. We will take a moment to name just a few of them.

The unavailable. They died before we forgave them. Or, they are hiding within an organization where we can't get to them.

Parents. Oscar Wilde wrote, "Children begin by loving their parents. After a time they judge them. Rarely, if ever, do they forgive them."

People who don't care. They tell us we can keep our forgiveness. They have no desire to work at a relationship.

They cut us off.

Ourselves. We judge, we convict and we sentence ourselves – mostly in secret. We struggle trying to play both the role of forgiver and forgiven.

The hideous. They are monsters. They trample people or treat them like playthings. They are sometimes ordinary people who commit extraordinarily evil acts.

God. He did not give us the answer we wanted to our prayers. He "took" someone we cared about deeply. He could have helped us, but He didn't.

I am certain that just the mention of these "challenging" opportunities for forgiveness will cause some readers to be frustrated with me for not providing satisfying answers. The truth is, I still have a lot to learn about forgiveness, myself. My writing about the subject is not due to my mastery of it; I only know that it is the way, the desire, and the heart of the Father. As is true of all of the subjects I discuss in this book, I am on the journey with you.

The English novelist Charles Williams remarked that forgiving is really a game; we can only play at it, he said, essentially we cannot do it. I disagree. More importantly, God disagrees, or else He would not command us to do it.

Forgiveness Within The Family

It has often been said that the people we hurt the most, are the people we love the most. If there is any truth to that statement, then learning to forgive family members is vitally important, although often more challenging.

There are so many possible scenarios where family members may hurt one another, due to all the relationships involved - between siblings and siblings, parents and children, spouses in marriage, grandparents, in-laws, extended family – on and on. Things get even stickier when people within the family begin to "take sides" during family spats.

Perhaps we are more relaxed around family, and therefore more careless with our behavior and with our words. Maybe the temptation to hurt a family member is stronger because of the information we may know about their history and their faults. It could be that family members are just convenient targets when we release our anger.

On the positive side, when we do what is required and forgive family members, we create a stronger, healthier environment in which the Father can be at work and can be glorified.

Church Feuds

Church members over the years have asked me, "If you had to name one sin of the Church that you most consistently see as you travel about speaking, which sin would you choose?" Tough question, but I believe I would have to choose the sin of unforgiveness.

Often overlooked is the unforgiveness between local ministers. Someone said something critical of another. Someone did not include another by inviting them to a particular function or meeting. Someone was perceived as influencing a family to leave one church and join another. Someone did not participate in taking a stand concerning a local community issue. Someone was discourteous or overlooked another while organizing or conducting a funeral service.

Also overlooked is the unforgiveness that exists on the occasion of a "church split." After the circus is over and the two new congregations have finished fighting, too often the need to provide healing through a service of reconciliation is ignored. The number of churches that exist today resulting from a church split is alarming to begin with, but there is simply no excuse for one church refusing to intentionally forgive another following a disagreement.

Somehow families within the church have found an environment in which it is easy to fight with other families. It is not unusual, particularly in smaller churches, to find a modern-day "Hatfields and McCoys" feud that has lasted for years. Add to all of this the unforgiveness existing between a former pastor who left in an atmosphere of tension and certain church members, and we have only just begun quite a list.

The Method Behind the Madness

The church family is made up of little children, young men and fathers. There are weak and strong Christians. There are some in need of milk and some in need of strong meat. There are some who need to be taught and some who need to teach.

Within the church family, relationships are often not given the care they require. Surely we have the biblical understanding of why that is so, from a spiritual warfare perspective. The devil is not "making" us misbehave in Church, but he is certainly relentless at the task of "instigating" division and discord among the children of God. If we give in to his temptation to fight against each other and to refuse to forgive each other (instead of resisting and fighting him), we end up with a dysfunctional church family.

In many American families, children and adults have a "role" they play at home. They assume various responsibilities, or "chores." They "help out" in a specific area for the benefit of the entire family. But in the Church, unless you are asked to serve on a "committee," the majority of members are unsure of their "role" and of where they "fit in." The result can be confusion and frustration among the family members.

My observation is that the majority of believers do not understand what their role is within the church family. Interestingly, one of the things that hinders forgiveness within the Church is our lack of knowledge regarding Spiritual Gifts. Does that sound strange to you?

Church members do not understand themselves (or one another) very well when it comes to spiritual job descriptions. Knowing, understanding and operating in our Spiritual Gifts dramatically increases our understanding of *why* fellow church members behave like they do, thus decreasing tension and criticism in relationships.

A church study of Spiritual Gifts will not, by itself, guarantee widespread forgiveness throughout the congregation – but it can be a very effective proactive step in that direction, not to mention the benefit to each individual member of discovering and understanding their own Gifts.

If the world is going to know we are Christians by our love, those who are watching need to see the fruits of unity and forgiveness operating among ministers and within the Church.

Thanks Be to God

Throughout his Christian life, the Apostle Paul never lost his sense of wonder at the thought of his own forgiveness. Paul told Timothy that previously he was a blasphemer and a persecutor, but had now obtained mercy. To be both forgiven and trusted by Someone such as Jesus caused Paul to marvel. I'm thinking that you and I should also be in awe that the Father, through His Son, has forgiven us.

What Is Clear?
Forgiveness is simply not optional – for me,
for my family and for my church!

What Motivates God?

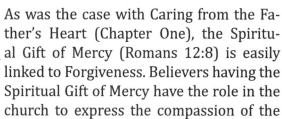 For the purpose of honoring and glorifying the Father, take some time right now and allow the Holy Spirit to reveal some relationships where your forgiveness is needed. First, examine your own relationships: to yourself, friends, family, church, and to God.

Second, intercede for relationships you are aware of where reconciliation or forgiveness is needed between people other than yourself – concerning communities, nations, organizations, churches, former pastors, family or friends.

When you have finished these prayers, ask the Father to *bless and strengthen* each of the relationships.

As was the case with Caring from the Father's Heart (Chapter One), the Spiritual Gift of Mercy (Romans 12:8) is easily linked to Forgiveness. Believers having the Spiritual Gift of Mercy have the role in the church to express the compassion of the Father's heart in a variety of ways. They have the ability to feel genuine empathy and compassion for individuals who are suffering physically, emotionally or spiritually. They act with supernatural ability on the opportunity to alleviate suffering.

Believers with the Spiritual Gift of Mercy feel supernaturally motivated to take part in or to establish ministries such as: Benevolence ministry, Food closet, Hospital visitation, Crisis pregnancy ministry, Homeless ministry, Widows/widowers ministry, Single parent ministry, Prison ministry, Senior adult ministry and Roadside prayer ministry

Usually Does

Too Often Does Not

PERSONAL REPORT CARD

_____ _____ Works at forgiving others, even the "difficult cases"

_____ _____ Remembers to thank God for His forgiveness through Christ

_____ _____ Remembers that past, present and future sins were forgiven at Calvary

_____ _____ Tries to complete each of the five "steps" of forgiveness

FAMILY REPORT CARD

_____ _____ Sees the importance of forgiving family members

_____ _____ Takes the initiative to forgive when hurt occurs in the family

_____ _____ Refrains from keeping a record of wrongs

_____ _____ Discerns and resists the devil's attempts to bring discord into the family

CHURCH REPORT CARD

_____ _____ Pastor models forgiveness by his behavior

_____ _____ Church members and families ask one another's forgiveness

_____ _____ Church has forgiven other churches with whom there has been previous conflict

_____ _____ Members have a good understanding of their roles and of Spiritual Gifts

What Motivates God?

Notes On "Forgiving from The Father's Heart"

_____

_____

_____

_____

_____

_____

_____

_____

_____

_____

_____

_____

_____

_____

_____

_____

_____

_____

_____

_____

Journal Of Turning Points

"To him who knows to do good and does not do it, to him it is sin." (James 4:17)

DATE | COMMITMENT

_____

_____

_____

_____

_____

_____

_____

"Hell is truth seen too late."

- Attributed to Tryon Edwards

Chapter Eight

Loving from The Father's Heart

"For God so loved the world that He gave His only begotten Son, that whoever believes in Him should not perish but have everlasting life."

- John 3:16

We come finally to focus on the last of eight specific roles that the Father desires to perform perfectly in the lives of His children. Some might say that this is the role from which all of the other roles are birthed, or that loving is the Father's "primary" role.

The first seven words, of what is probably the most well known verse of Scripture to mankind – John 3:16 – are, without a doubt, the most overlooked. Yet these seven words explain "why" the Father would do such an incredible thing – because He "*so loved*." Pierre Vinet made this revealing statement, "The Christian faith does not consist in the belief that we are saved, but in the belief that we are loved."

The objects of the Father's love include those who love Christ, and those who believe in the Savior's divine mission. The Church, therefore, should consist of people who love Jesus, and who express that love through growing the kingdom of God on earth.

What do we know about the *character* of the Father's love?

- It is Self-declared (a free promise on His part)
- It has existed from the very first
- It is constant and unceasing
- It is gracious and undeserved
- It is merciful and righteous in its purpose

What Motivates God?

In God's loving hands, and in His hands only, are the matters of life and death, of sickness and health. Let us consider a portion of Hezekiah's prayer of praise and gratitude recorded in Isaiah 38:17: "*But You have lovingly delivered my soul from the pit of corruption, for You have cast all my sins behind Your back.*" Hallelujah! O, what if I had gone to the pit? But, because of His love, my sins are not before His face but behind His back! He sees them no more!

Matthew Henry wrote, "When we cast our sins behind our back, and take no care to repent of them, God sets them before His face, and is ready to reckon for them; but when we set them before our face, in true repentance, as David did when his sin was ever before him, God casts them behind His back." This is why we marvel at grace: That God would treat His people as if they were not sinners!

God's Love, The Early Church and Redemption

God created the world with the desire to have a body of pure, good, happy, intelligent worshippers dwelling with him in heaven for all eternity. But knowing that man would fall, He determined from the first that He would raise up a certain number out of fallen humanity – save and purify them – and make them His "peculiar people," "*a people for Himself*" (Deuteronomy 14:2), His Church.

It could be said, then, that God loved His Church "by anticipation," before He had created it. Jesus spoke of the Church (Matthew 18:17) before it had actually "formed," so it is clear that the Church was on the Father's heart from the start. And He most certainly showed (and continues to show) His love and care for the Church by ceaseless watchfulness, supernatural interventions, timely warnings, divine guidance, Holy Spirit teaching and amazing patience!

This Church He has built upon a rock, promised to be with it always, and declared that the gates of hell will not prevail against it. He "*nourishes and cherishes it*" (Ephesians

5:29), and protects it from both clear and secret enemies and all attempts to crush and destroy it.

The early church eventually came to the realization, as they looked back, that the crucifixion was actually the *love* of God dealing with the sins of men, offering them forgiveness and a new beginning if they would only come and accept it. They began to understand that the Cross was about the love of God Himself.

In this light, the church became a new kind of community; it was a society of sinners forgiven who began confessing, "Not I, but the grace of God." Barriers between men began to break down. The members grew to love each other because God first loved them, and drew them out of themselves into the unity of "one body." We now had the new People of God, the new Israel, the *Ecclesia*, the Body of Christ, the Church.

Today's Church, like the early church, needs to see the value that the Father has placed on man, and to see the place of man in the Father's eternal purpose. In short, we too, need to see the meaning of Jesus' redemptive work.

Romans 3:24-25 says that Christ Jesus, *"whom God set forth as a propitiation by His blood,"* provided redemption on the ground of which sinners, who put their faith in Him, are justified. The experience of being redeemed results in our belonging to a holy God, obliging us to seek holiness of life (1 Corinthians 6:18-20, 7:23; 1 Peter 1:14-19).

Herbert Lockyer, writing on the Doctrine of Redemption in his book, *All The Doctrines of The Bible*, says: "Among the cardinal truths of our Christian faith, none demands our prayerful and intelligent consideration as that of redemption. In its broadest sense, redemption covers the entire work of God in Christ, delivering man from the guilt and government, penalty and presence of sin."

May you and I never, ever be ashamed to testify of His redeeming grace! *"Let the redeemed of the Lord say so"* (Psalm 107:2).

The Compassion of Jesus for Mankind

In both the Introduction and Chapter One of this book, I referenced Matthew 9:36 when mentioning our Lord's compassion for people. We return to that verse once again, this time for a more precise description of what Jesus saw when he looked at this multitude.

The tense of the words describing the "sheep" Jesus pictured indicates that their present condition was the result of a past act. When sheep wander among brambles and sharp rocks, their skin gets torn. Jesus saw people resembling sheep that were exhausted from contact with the sharpness of life. The people before His eyes appeared to be physically, emotionally and spiritually, thrown down prone and helpless. The verb used here is used with reference to corpses lying prostrate on the ground. Loving from the Father's heart, seeing with the Father's eyes, revealed a torn and exhausted flock. Jesus was *"moved"* by what He saw.

Jesus insisted that those who profess to serve the Father must be equally compassionate (Matthew 5:43-48). He is merciful, and we must be merciful too (Luke 6:36). Jesus' ministry to men was the outcome of His love for men. Unless man becomes the object of our affection, we cannot possibly become a servant of men. How can we but hold men dear when we know their worth to the Lord?

It grieves me that the Church still tries to find *methods* that will "move" God's people into service. *Methods do not move people; love moves people!* And you and I will minister to others as we should – only when we develop a heart like our Savior's that can see spiritual distress. May each of us walk closer to Him today than we did yesterday, that we may increasingly have His heart!

How God's Love Should Move Us

It is an amazing thing, a disturbing thing, that such a large number of believers have little concern for men. Interest in and compassion for the human race (not for just a certain section of it) is a basic requirement of every Christian. The Father's love includes all men, and so should ours. How can anyone be used to save souls, who does not *love* souls?

The attitude of our own hearts is sometimes the hindrance. Believers should not move about among men giving the impression that they are doing people a favor by just shaking their hand. You and I should be relating to everyone in such a way that we never make a person feel that we are different from him or her. An ignorant, unsaved man differs from you and me in no other respect than that we are saved and he is not. We should not need to take a course in evangelism to realize that!

Here's the "bottom line." If we seek the lost because we have come to see how precious every single soul is to the Father, then we will be "moved" to them – not because someone made us feel guilty, or manipulated us into doing it, or we took part in a special emphasis, or we heard it preached one hundred times – but because of *an irresistible attraction birthed out of His love!*

Jesus commanded us to "*love one another as I have loved you*" (John 15:12), and 1 John 4:11 says, "*Beloved, if God so loved us, we also ought to love one another.*" If believers do not learn to love one another, how will we ever learn to love lost souls? And how will we ever learn to love our enemies?

Paul wrote to the Philippians how much he loved them and longed for them all, "*with the affection of Jesus Christ*" (Philippians 1:8). His pulse was beating with the pulse of Christ; his heart was throbbing with the heart of Christ. Paul came to such a depth in his union with Christ, that Jesus' heart had taken possession of his heart! Ah! For many of us this condition seems so far out of reach, but it is not! We have become *"partakers of the divine nature"* (2 Peter 1:4). The remainder of our earthly life is an outworking of what God has already "in-worked."

We are called to become what we are.

We are to love others with the tender feelings of the Father's love, because He made them and because Christ died for them. Warren Wiersbe has written, "The closer we grow to the Lord, the more of His love we will want to share with others. Christian love is simply treating others the way God has treated us. God has forgiven us, so we forgive others. God meets our needs, so we try to help meet the needs of others. God listens when we speak to Him, so we listen when people speak to us. Christian love is seen in our attitudes and our actions; otherwise what we think is 'love' is only shallow sentiment."

As we think about the Father's love moving us, two characteristics of His love should become characteristics of ours. The first is that His love is *unchanging*. His love does not vary. Our love is often fickle and fluctuates depending on how people treat us. The second characteristic is that His love is *gracious*. The love and "favor" of God are inseparable. It ought to be said of all believers: "He never meets a stranger." Strangers should feel comfortable and accepted when they meet a Christian. For Jesus' sake, you can be a friend to every stranger you meet.

Your family should seek to manifest the heart of the Father to a lost world. You can sit down together and discuss ways to put people ahead of family routines that are self-serving. If your family believes that people are the Father's most valued creation, is this belief reflected in the way your family spends the majority of its time? With careful planning, your family can enjoy quality time together and still be intentional about participating in neighborhood, local and foreign missions.

Friendships and marriage relationships are clearly a place where loving from the Father's heart is applicable. A. A. Milne put it this way: "In all your thoughts, and in all your acts, in every hope and in every fear, when you soar to the skies and when you fall to the ground, always you are holding the other person's hand."

The Father's Love and The Church

Here are a couple of examples in church life where we can practice loving with the Father's heart "inside the walls." The first area is in the way we show the Father's love to the pastor and staff. Having served in the local church as both a pastor and staff person myself, I know how it feels to be on the "other side" of this one.

"Pastor Appreciation Day" is nice, and if your church does not already have such a day (or week), you should establish one and make it an annual observance from now on. But Pastor Appreciation Day is like "Mother's Day," in that we need to make sure that special people feel loved on the rest of the days of the year as well.

Trust me, even the best pastors receive more words of criticism or complaint than they do words of praise or appreciation. I still have the cards and notes expressing love from church members that were written to me many years ago. Please, consider taking the time to give your pastor a hand-written note or card, take him and his wife out to dinner, or express your love and appreciation to him in some intentional and significant way. And, above all, *pray for him and his family daily!*

Second, Ephesians 4:15 contains the important words, *"Speaking the truth in love."* Whether we are in the pulpit or the parking lot of the church, there is generally room for improvement here. Without a doubt, the church house is a place where God's truth should be communicated. But some of the best sermons I have ever heard were ruined because truth was communicated clearly, but love was not.

We can all work on the tone of our voice and our body language to insure that we convey the love of the Father when we are speaking the truth. We can guard against correcting people with the truth when we are hurt or mad – *especially* from the pulpit. And we can be careful of our "timing" when we choose to speak the truth lovingly, giving consideration to the listener's feelings or circumstances.

"Outside the walls" we should leave the Father's love wherever we go. Jesus did this *so* beautifully – when He fed the hungry, when He healed the sick, when He encouraged the lonely, when He forgave sin or when He visited a home. Every time we say or do something in Jesus' name, individually or as the Church, the people we come into contact with should sense the presence of God when we leave.

Jesus loves everyone, including those we may not love. We may not understand people, but we can love them. We have absolutely no right to hate people just because they are of a different race, political party, or religious denomination or faith. We must intentionally love others with the Father's heart whether we are communicating as a family, in the workplace, as a community, or even as a nation to a world that needs Jesus.

The Connection Between Love and Obedience

Motivation is the stimulus that causes us to do something. And the highest motivation for obedience is love. Whatever or whomever you love in life, will motivate you. The truth of these statements is seen in Scripture. Jesus said, "*If you love Me, [you will] keep my commandments*" (John 14:15). 1 John 5:3 says, "*For this is the love of God, that we keep His commandments.*"

Notice the use of the word "keep" in each of these verses. Anyone can obey on occasions when it is easy to do so, or when it does not cost to obey. But if we are to keep His commandments, *loyalty* is involved. Love for the Father is not so much an emotional experience, as it is real activity expressed through sacrificial service.

What are the connections between love and obedience? There are several. First, love establishes a personal relationship with the Father. The Father understands our human frailty. Psalm 103:14 says, *"For He knows our frame; He remembers that we are dust."* Therefore, He knows how much we need His fatherly compassion. No matter what the Father gives or withholds, love centers around the giver rather than the gift. Job declared, *"Though He slay me, yet will I trust Him"* (Job 13:15).

Second, the Father gives us commands because He loves us. Remember, God is love (1 John 4:8). There is no need to question God's commandments because, *"There is no fear in love"* (1 John 4:18). Jesus said, *"He who has my commandments and keeps them, it is he who loves me. And he who loves Me will be loved by My Father, and I will love him and manifest Myself to him."*

Third, if we love the Father, we do not count or measure the cost of obedience; we just obey. Love that calculates is not true love. Jesus proved His love for us by going to the Cross for us and by giving us His all.

Obedience from the heart is what the Father desires. Do you know what book of the Torah Jesus quoted from more than any other? You may be surprised to learn that it was Deuteronomy! And in the New Testament, Deuteronomy is quoted or referred to over eighty times. Why? Deuteronomy emphasizes the *heart*; it is the book of loving obedience and obedient love.

Fact: To know Him is to love Him. And the more we love Him, the more we will obey Him.

What Motivates God?

Love's Great Question

"Simon, son of Jonah, do you love Me?" (John 21:17). It is not difficult to find people who will say they love Jesus. But it is rare to find people who love Him *supremely*. Peter loved Jesus. He was sincere, but he did not understand the weakness of his own love.

Sometimes we want to know the love of Jesus without *belonging* to Him. *"To know the love of Christ"* (Ephesians 3:19) we must begin by making Him our first love.

The true test of our love is not what we say with our lips, but rather, when we are torn, when we are tested, tempted and tried – and *still*, we stand close to His side. When have you and I proved to Jesus and to ourselves, that we love Him supremely? Someday He may look at one of us and ask, "Do you love Me?" What if it is today? Are we listening?

"What Motivates God?" is another penetrating question. Being perfect, God would not seem to need motivation to do *anything*. Zophar asked Job, *"Can you search out the deep things of God? Can you find out the limits of the Almighty?"* (Job 11:7). God being holy and infinite, the answer is obviously, "no." Yet, given His intimate relationship to His children, the Church and mankind, we have sought in this book to show that there is, in fact, some inherent "motivation" that persuades God to provide for all of us so completely: His desire to be a *perfect Father!*

The degree to which we know and understand God and His heart determines everything about us...as individuals, as families, and as the Church. We respond to the God that we know.

This book has been written with the conviction that we as believers must thoroughly understand the meaning and significance of God's primary roles, and then intentionally *let those same roles manifest* in our lives, in our families, and in the Church.

A Prayer for The Church

Before Solomon dedicated the temple, he prayed a precious prayer recorded in 2 Chronicles 6:40-42. Verse 41 records the following portion of his prayer: "*Let Your priests, O Lord God, be clothed with salvation, and let Your saints rejoice in goodness.*"

The "*priests,*" the ministers of the church, are to be prayed for: that they may "*be clothed with salvation.*" This means praying specifically for our ministers to be upright, sincere men of integrity in their hearts before God... virtuous and correct in their walk before men (see Chapter Six of this book). It means praying for our pastors and teachers to be absorbed in the work of soul winning and discipling.

The "*saints,*" separated, holy believers beloved for Christ's sake, are to be prayed for: that they may "*rejoice in goodness.*" This means praying specifically for church members to live in the joy of the Lord and in goodness of the highest sense. It means praying for ourselves and for fellow believers to exhibit the Father's heart by caring, listening and forgiving, as we have seen in previous chapters of this book.

As I prepare to send this book out into the world, my prayer for you, your family, and your church is that you will *let people see the Father's heart!*

What Is Clear?

I need to be so overwhelmed by God's love that I am moved with compassion to share it with everyone!

Pray that your love for all men would deepen to the place where you are in continuous intercession for lost souls. It may help you to begin the discipline of keeping a prayer journal where you list the names of lost people for whom you are burdened. Pray the Scripture found in 1 Timothy 2:1-5.

If you have not done so already, place your pastor, staff members and leaders on your personal prayer list. Pray that the Father will keep them holy and pure and in sweet fellowship with Him.

Pray constantly for fellow believers by name. Pray that you will remember to see the spiritual connection between love and obedience.

Believers with the Spiritual Gift of Exhortation (Romans 12:8) have the role in the church of ministering words of comfort, consolation, encouragement or counsel to other church members in such a way that they feel helped or healed. These Christians are supernaturally motivated to "come alongside" to help, strengthen, steady, reassure and console. They are more patient with slow progress than most of us, and they enjoy stimulating the faith of others.

If you have the Spiritual Gift of Exhortation you may enjoy taking part in such ministries as: Counseling, Distressed teens/battered women, Outreach, Prayer teams, New Christian mentor, Youth work, Youth camp counselor, Mentally/physically challenged, Homebound ministry, or Hospital visitation.

Usually Does Too Often Does Not

PERSONAL REPORT CARD

_____ _____ Invites lost people to church services

_____ _____ Speaks and behaves in a manner that demonstrates God's love

_____ _____ Shares the Father's love through conversation and lifestyle

_____ _____ Prays regularly for the salvation of specific people

FAMILY REPORT CARD

_____ _____ Looks for opportunities to be a witness as a family

_____ _____ Offers encouragement and support to each other to be a more effective witness

_____ _____ Relates to neighbors in such a way that demonstrates the Father's love

_____ _____ Prays for the salvation of entire families who live in the area

CHURCH REPORT CARD

_____ _____ Church budget reflects a clear expression of God's love to the community and the world

_____ _____ Teaching, preaching and music proclaims the Father's love

_____ _____ Joins with other churches to reach the community for Christ

_____ _____ Stresses the desire for only God to receive glory

What Motivates God?

Notes On "Loving from The Father's Heart"

Journal Of Turning Points

"To him who knows to do good and does not do it, to him it is sin." (James 4:17)

DATE | COMMITMENT

_____

_____

_____

_____

_____

_____

_____

Index of References to Holy Scripture

OLD TESTAMENT

What Motivates God?

NEW TESTAMENT

Matthew

Mark

Luke

John

Acts

Romans

What Motivates God?

Invite Rick Astle To Teach At Your Church!

If the Father has blessed you through reading this book, you may want to pray about inviting Rick to come and teach this material at your church. Local church and area-wide conferences are a key feature of Rick Astle Ministries. You can contact Rick to schedule a conference by e-mailing him at rick@rickastle.com

Have A Kingdom-Focused Week!

See a new kingdom-focused prayer prompt and a new spiritual awakening quote every week from Rick, by following him on twitter: @astleministries, or by visiting his website at www.RickAstle.com

What Motivates God?